MW00815200

PRAISE FOR *SERVING EDUCATION/ A FIVE-COURSE FRAMEWORK FOR ACCELERATED LEARNING*

"This book presents an excellent step-by-step approach to a difficult concept and a clever, logical, go-to approach to integrating educational equity into teaching and student/family interaction. The use of scenarios helps teachers to relate to the discussions and approaches quickly. The format is accessible for an overworked teacher to pick up and implement quickly. With its many references and graphics, it will open new doors for those teachers who 'knew' that something was missing in reaching all their students. I recommend this book to all classroom teachers, administrators, and teacher educators; it is a rich accumulation of wisdom, experience, and logical thinking about a topic that is often misconceived or avoided."

Dr. Jacquelyn A. Lewis-Harris
Associate Professor, University of Missouri—St. Louis,
College of Education (Retired)
Former Director of the Connecting Human Origin and
Cultural Diversity Program

"*Serving Educational Equity* supports educators challenged by disrupted student learning. This timely new book guides educators on their journey for educational equity. Murray-Darden and Turner successfully developed an accessible resource for teachers, instructional leaders, and coaches established on evidence-based research centered on equity-focused practices. *Serving Educational Equity* offers readers the tools and strategies for educator self-reflection needed for them to develop the mindset to ensure that all students can learn and achieve."

Dr. Karen I. Hall, Assistant Professor
Saint Louis University, School of Education, St. Louis, MO

"*Serving Educational Equity* is the book teachers have been looking for. It synthesizes all the best practices that are applicable to current teaching and learning while providing manageable explanations and connections across what may have been incorrectly perceived as unrelated concepts. Get ready to have all the dots connect!"

Saundra Mouton
International Baccalaureate Primary Years Programme Coordinator and Assistant
Principal
Briarmeadow Charter School & Barbara Bush Elementary
Houston, TX

"The book provides a ton of practical visuals and tools that leadership teams can use in their schools... a great guide for meaningful discussion and professional growth."

Dr. Jacie Maslyk, Instructional Coach and Consultant
Pittsburgh, PA

"This book would be an excellent choice as the foundation for a collaborative book study designed to strengthen teams of educators."

Lena Marie Rockwood
Assistant Principal for Student Success
Revere High School, Revere, MA

"This book is a must-read for educators! In fact, it is one of the best education books I have ever read! The topic of unfinished learning through acceleration will provide you with the needed support for student success. Each phase includes valuable vignettes, many resources, and much more."

Dr. Ronda Gray, Clinical Associate Professor
School of Education, University of Illinois at Springfield
Springfield, IL

"*Serving Educational Equity* is essential reading for school personnel. The authors provide the strategies, research, tools and resources, based on their incredible experiences, to address the old chestnut—lost learning and student achievement. This will become your new school handbook!"

Dr. Ken Darvall, Principal
Tema International School, Tema, Ghana

"Students and educators have been through some difficult times these past few years, which has given us an opportunity for educators to take a renewed look at their practice. This book provides the reader with a fresh perspective for rejuvenation."

Cathy Patterson, Retired Elementary Educator/AP
Walnut Valley Unified School District, Walnut, CA

"The book is highly comprehensive in covering the various aspects of teaching and learning that impact on equity and inclusion... It's the kind of book you will come back to over and over again, getting different insights as you go through the questions at different times in your life."

Rachael Lehr, Associate Principal
Dayton Primary School, Perth, Western Australia

SERVING EDUCATIONAL EQUITY

This book is dedicated to my late father, Charles A. Murray, Sr. Thank you for being my first storyteller. Your light will forever shine in my heart. Thank you, mom, Shirley Murray, for being an example of style and grace. I dedicate this book to my family for your unwavering commitment and support of my endeavors. This book is for the students and educators whose stories beautifully grace the pages.
Sonya

We dedicate this book to our families for always supporting our personal and professional endeavors. We dedicate this book to our students and educators who have shared their lives and dreams.
Gwen

SERVING EDUCATIONAL EQUITY

A Five-Course Framework for Accelerated Learning

SONYA MURRAY-DARDEN

GWENDOLYN Y. TURNER

FOREWORD BY
BARBARA R. BLACKBURN

FOR INFORMATION:

Corwin
A SAGE Company
2455 Teller Road
Thousand Oaks, California 91320
(800) 233-9936
www.corwin.com

SAGE Publications Ltd.
1 Oliver's Yard
55 City Road
London EC1Y 1SP
United Kingdom

SAGE Publications India Pvt. Ltd.
Unit No 323-333, Third Floor, F-Block
International Trade Tower Nehru Place
New Delhi 110 019
India

SAGE Publications Asia-Pacific Pte. Ltd.
18 Cross Street #10-10/11/12
China Square Central
Singapore 048423

President: Mike Soules
Vice President and Editorial Director:
    Monica Eckman
Acquisitions Editor: Megan Bedell
Senior Content Development Editor:
    Lucas Schleicher
Content Development Editor:
    Mia Rodriguez
Editorial Assistant: Natalie Delpino
Production Editor: Vijayakumar
Copy Editor: Christobel Colleen Hopman
Typesetter: TNQ Technologies
Proofreader: Benny Willy Stephen
Indexer: TNQ Technologies
Cover Designer: Janet Kiesel
Marketing Manager: Melissa Duclos

Printed in Canada

Library of Congress Cataloging-in-Publication Data

Names: Murray-Darden, Sonya, author. | Turner, Gwendolyn Yvonne, author.

Title: Serving educational equity : a five-course framework for accelerated learning / Sonya Murray-Darden, Gwendolyn Y. Turner.

Description: First edition. | Thousand Oaks, California : Corwin, [2023] | Includes bibliographical references and index.

Identifiers: LCCN 2023015546 | ISBN 9781071909478 (paperback : acid-free paper) | ISBN 9781071909508 (adobe pdf) | ISBN 9781071909485 (epub) | ISBN 9781071909492 (epub)

Subjects: LCSH: Educational acceleration —United States —Handbooks, manuals, etc. | Educational equalization —United States.

Classification: LCC LB1029.A22 M87 2023 | DDC 379.2/60973 —dc23/eng/20230411

LC record available at https://lccn.loc.gov/2023015546

This book is printed on acid-free paper.

23 24 25 26 27 10 9 8 7 6 5 4 3 2 1

CONTENTS

FOREWORD

When I was asked to write a foreword for *Serving Educational Equity: A Five-Course Framework for Accelerated Learning*, I was simultaneously intrigued and excited. I was intrigued because I've been looking for a comprehensive, practical approach to focusing on equity in terms of moving students forward (acceleration), not just bringing them to an "equal place (remediation)." I was excited because once I started reading, I couldn't stop. Finally, someone was focused on what teachers could control… what they could actually do in their classrooms, whether or not there was a larger focus outside their classrooms.

With a strong research-based foundation, Sonya Murray-Darden and Gwendolyn Turner provide recommendations for classroom practices ranging from planning, self-awareness of biases, ensuring student voice, equitable instruction, and engagement. While they build their work on the *Science of Learning Development (SoLD)* as a framework, additional research informs their work throughout the book. Using the metaphor of a five-course meal for their suggestions allows them to link all aspects of the instructional practices together in a coherent, yet understandable manner. This is only enhanced by the practical stories from educators that are scattered throughout the text. Their approach truly epitomizes moving students to higher levels of rigor through a lens of equity.

Barbara R. Blackburn, PhD
bcgroup@gmail.com

INTRODUCTION

In many ways, this book is over 20 years in the making, initiated from a friendship and mentorship in St. Louis, Missouri. Our journey as veteran educators, who have coached, mentored, and taught countless school leaders, teachers, and students in districts across the country, led us to believe that we need to reimagine how we guide students to educational excellence. For years, educators have asked for a playbook of resources to help them better meet their students' academic foundational needs and help prepare them for a more inclusive society. Educators' desire for sound teaching practices and learning strategies fed our passion for creating a comprehensive book of evidence-based techniques, practical approaches, and effective methods to address unfinished learning and promote equity engagement. This book provides instructional leaders and coaches with a sound theoretical framework for addressing unfinished learning and teaching.

Serving Educational Equity is rooted in tenets of equity, accelerated teaching, and a "whole child" approach to student learning and engagement. We believe that to embrace equity as an avenue to learning acceleration our schools must provide systems, supportive environments, productive instructional strategies, and social and emotional development so that learners can persevere as they engage in meaningful learning experiences. Therefore, the book draws on the theoretical principles outlined in the Science of Learning Development (*SoLD*) principles (Darling-Hammond et al., 2020). The *Science of Learning and Development (SoLD) Principles* serve as the theoretical framework for our work because they focus on the academic, cognitive, ethical, physical, psychological, and social-emotional development of the whole child. Furthermore, as we explore the connections between equity and learning, throughout this book, we embrace the following concepts on how people learn effectively from the Learning Policy Institute (Darling-Hammond & Edgerton, 2021):

The brain is always developing as a product of relationships and experiences.

- Learning is social, emotional, and academic.
- Students' perceptions of their own ability and their level of trust in their environment influence learning.
- Supportive, developmental relationships are the most effective antidote to trauma. (The Learning Policy Institute, 2021)

The National Equity Project (2022) defines *educational equity as helping each child receive what they need to develop to their full academic and social potential. Working towards equity in schools involves ensuring equally high outcomes for all participants within the educational system, removing the predictability of success or failures that currently correlates with any social or cultural factor. Specifically, it means interrupting inequitable practices, examining biases, creating inclusive multicultural school environments for adults and children, and discovering and cultivating every human's unique gifts, talents, and interests.*

Serving Educational Equity serves as a resource for persons interested in accelerating and advancing the educational needs of all learners. Acceleration may be defined as "preparing students for new learning and getting them ready for success in the present" and does not concentrate on a litany of items that students have failed to master (Pepper-Rollins, 2014). We discuss the importance of connecting our *"why"* to student equity, excellence, and acceleration.

To effectively accelerate student learning, educators will want to understand and address the needs of the whole child. The Learning Policy Institute (2022) defines a *"whole child" education as prioritizing the full scope of a child's developmental needs to advance educational equity and ensure that every child reaches their fullest potential. A whole child approach understands that students' education and life outcomes depend upon their access to more profound learning opportunities in and out of school and their school environment and relationships.*

Serving Educational Equity is needed because school officials desire to advance students' learning as a matter of educational equity. Our book is unique in that we connect equity and acceleration as primary elements in advancing students' learning. This book offers a practical approach to educational equity that starts with self-reflection and transitions to relevant action. We offer educators what they have desired: a clear approach rooted in scientifically based practices to advancing students' learning. In our experiences around the country, we have found that despite different locations and communities, the issues were the same; each educator at the school and leader level wanted strategies for helping students find success. Unfortunately, many educators sought the nonrealistic vision of quick fixes or silver bullets. Instead, it was apparent that careful consideration of evidence-based, situational strategies, data, and strategic planning can make a difference. As we worked alongside teachers and leaders, it became clear that the work of equity lies in assessing the school for situational awareness and in self-reflection on what is possible. It is for these reasons

Serving Educational Equity was written. We wish to provide a menu for others interested in embarking upon the journey of educational equity for every child.

THE DRIVING FORCE: START WITH THE *"WHY"*

In 2009, Simon Sinek started a movement to inspire people to start with their "why" to embrace adaptive change. In his best-selling book, *Starting With the Why*, Simon Sinek reminds us that our "why" is the purpose, cause, or belief that helps us do what we need to do to make change (Sinek, 2009). Since then, millions of people have been touched by his theory. Traditionally, educators start with the "what" and the "how" of teaching and learning. Transformational change at the reimagined teaching and learning level must come from our "why" and a deep place within us, a place we hold close when the going gets tough. Our motivation for educational excellence is the driving force for our "why." Every student deserves educators who want them to excel and achieve at high levels. That is why we wrote this book, to offer practical strategies that support educators as they engage in the work of equity and acceleration of teaching and learning.

ABOUT THE AUTHORS

Sonya Murray-Darden

My "why" has evolved throughout my experience serving students in numerous educational settings as a professional developer, classroom teacher, leadership coach, reading specialist, administrator, and researcher. But no experience shaped my why, like losing my former student who was shot and killed in Ferguson, Missouri. His death would spark public protests, social unrest, and outrage within my community and beyond, forcing much-needed conversations across the country about the role of social justice in schools.

Mike was a gentle soul who loved mathematics and was part of my reading club. There was much in the news media about his tragedy, but what I knew as his former teacher was that he loved mathematics even after graduating from high school. I wanted to think the teaching and learning he received and the information I poured into him as a student influenced his love of mathematics. Ironically, his tragedy occurred the same day I graduated from college with an advanced degree, causing me to reflect deeply on the external and internal influences of teaching and learning and my personal "why." As I pondered the many sacrifices of my parents and teachers and Mike's tragedy, I concluded that equity is about using education as a vessel to change lives. The educators I encountered influenced my life trajectory and educational experiences. My path began as a student in an urban school district with teachers who cared and provided the foundational learning I needed to succeed, but I didn't live in an area where schools were "considered" the best. My parents decided to transition my siblings and me to a desegregated school by eighth grade, riding a school bus for nearly an hour each way to a new school community. This community was very different from where I was raised and was considered "a better educational opportunity."

As I traveled across town to a school that offered more opportunities and access, the program offerings were better, but I felt isolated. I was invisible. The experience helped me understand the difference between "intent" and "impact." The school was challenging and rich in experiences, intending to diversify educational experiences for all students by offering more opportunities, yet the impact was a stifled voice. I quickly learned that serving equity requires elevating the voice of the underserved, choosing the right curriculum, understanding the impact of external influences, building relationships, and reflecting on the instructional decisions we implement when we elevate students' possibilities.

Ultimately, I founded Equity Matters Consulting, a consulting company focused on helping educators advance education by giving students a voice and a seat at the table. Our team focuses on adult learning theory to disrupt the status quo in schools and organizations using a practical, inspirational approach. I began testing parts of the serving educational equity framework with practitioners over the past few years. I assembled strategies from our recent day-to-day consulting experiences with schools and organizations to offer as best practices in this book.

Educational equity shines a spotlight on our expectations and asks us to reflect on how we hinder or elevate opportunities for students to have a better life. We should center a vision of excellence for every child, no matter their zip code, background, or linguistic ability. Our book supports practitioners with resources to operationalize educational equity using actionable practices that ensure educational equity for all students.

Gwendolyn Y. Turner

As an educator who has worked in numerous educational settings: classroom teacher, substitute teacher, reading specialist, adult educator, administrator, educational consultant, teacher educator, college professor, and researcher, I have learned to respect both the teaching and learning process. One can expect culturally, linguistically, and academically diverse students in any educational setting. My career as an educator started in a rural area and later with migrant populations, where very few economic advancement opportunities were available for families. These families taught me the importance of resiliency and the timeliness of quality, relevant educational experiences that allowed students to acquire problem-solving, reasoning, and critical thinking tools. These tools are essential in both academic and general life. We did not have time to waste on meaningless or irrelevant learning activities because a quality educational experience would be a ticket to greater life opportunities. When I started working with educators and visiting classrooms in Bolivia and Brazil, I realized that quality education does not just prepare students to complete school assignments but prepares them for all of their life experiences as adults, parents, employees, and citizens. In America, we take education for granted, but my experiences in schools and classrooms in South Africa and Thailand reinforced my belief that education changes lives. We serve students best by honoring their voices, acknowledging their identities, and valuing their life experiences. Students who receive quality education have many more life opportunities than those who receive an inferior education. Too often we provide the best educational resources, activities, and experiences for those already advantaged students. Equity is a lens that educators can use to ensure all students reach their full potential. I respect the teaching and learning process. I believe that quality education improves the quality of one's life. Lastly, I believe that as an educator, I can help students improve their life trajectories.

As I worked in suburban and urban educational settings, I realized that students enter a classroom expecting to learn, be engaged, and have their opinions and voices heard. My beliefs, practices, and actions can profoundly impact the learning success of students regardless of their academic abilities, cultural background, or linguistic ability. We are not helping students complete assignments for class; we are assisting students with the tools they need for success in their lives. This is why I have embraced educational equity throughout my career. I believe that educational equity provides opportunities for all students to soar academically.

Our work as educators is to help students acquire the tools they need for both careers and life. Therefore, we must provide instruction that meets students' academic and social needs. Respecting the rights of students to experience rich, meaningful learning experiences has been the cornerstone of my work as an educator. This is a lesson I have embraced in my work in this country and as a visiting instructor in Bolivia, Brazil, Thailand, and South Africa. Students want to learn and experience success while learning. All students deserve intellectually challenging, relevant, and engaging learning activities in a supportive environment. Education is still the key that unlocks opportunities for students now and in their futures.

OUTLINE OF THE BOOK

The analogy to planning a multicourse meal is used as the book's organizational format, offering comprehensive resources and multiple entry points for readers desiring educational equity. See Figure I.1. The design presents the authors' recipe for reimagining teaching and learning, ensuring students' educational equity and accelerated learning by utilizing an analogy for meal planning. Each chapter begins with a real-life scenario or issue that educators face in providing effective instruction and educational support for their students. In addition, each chapter is arranged so that the reader reflects on instructional and organizational challenges that serve as barriers to advancing academic excellence. We recognize the real-world complexities of schools and classrooms.

The multicourse framework to Equity and Acceleration we offer provides educators with a simple, memorable menu to accelerate all students' learning as a matter of equity. Each chapter summarizes the content as a course or phase, offers research and best practices, a scenario, and reflective questioning for readers that concludes with planning resources. Lists of resources are included at the end of each chapter and in the appendix. The content can be utilized at the classroom, building, and system levels. The multicourse approach functions: (a) To guide reimagination and instructional recovery efforts through a lens of educational equity. (b) To push the acceleration of students' learning as a more practical approach for addressing unfinished learning rather than remediation. (c) To aid efforts in meeting the academic needs of *all learners*.

Each chapter presents the planning, instruction, background, concepts, theoretical framework, methods, approaches, techniques, and evaluation strategies for implementing change and accelerating learning in the classroom. The chapters are organized as a menu of phases for planning, instructing, evaluating, and reflecting. Chapter 1: We ask the reader to embrace acceleration by assessing their current state of educational equity using a Strengths, Weaknesses, Opportunities, and Threats (SWOT) analysis of learning acceleration. Chapter 2: The reader reflects on best practices and the role relationships play in addressing trauma and socioemotional awareness in children. Chapter 3: The readers think about their curriculum and data strategy to address learning acceleration. Chapter 4: We raise the importance of recognizing students' voices for diversity and equity. Chapter 5 is analogous to the main course in meal planning, suggesting effective research-based

Figure I.1 • *Murray and Turner's (2021) Five-Course Framework for Accelerated Learning*

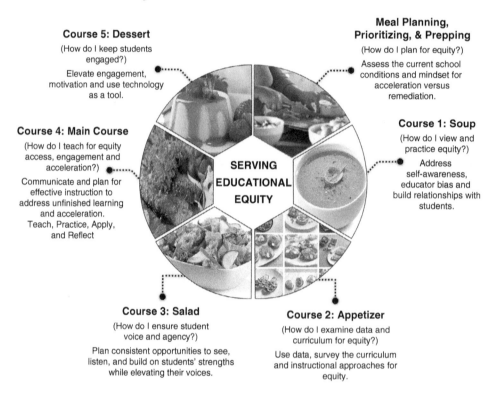

Course 5: Dessert
(How do I keep students engaged?)
Elevate engagement, motivation and use technology as a tool.

Meal Planning, Prioritizing, & Prepping
(How do I plan for equity?)
Assess the current school conditions and mindset for acceleration versus remediation.

Course 4: Main Course
(How do I teach for equity access, engagement and acceleration?)
Communicate and plan for effective instruction to address unfinished learning and acceleration.
Teach, Practice, Apply, and Reflect

SERVING EDUCATIONAL EQUITY

Course 1: Soup
(How do I view and practice equity?)
Address self-awareness, educator bias and build relationships with students.

Course 3: Salad
(How do I ensure student voice and agency?)
Plan consistent opportunities to see, listen, and build on students' strengths while elevating their voices.

Course 2: Appetizer
(How do I examine data and curriculum for equity?)
Use data, survey the curriculum and instructional approaches for equity.

instructional strategies and pedagogy for implementing effective instruction. The SoLD principles serve as the research base for our suggested ideas. We share pedagogical practices to ensure foundational readiness, address unfinished teaching and learning, and implement effective instruction. Chapter 6: The dessert chapter asks leaders to promote, expand, and reflect on engagement and to motivate all students in the digital world. We provide readily available digital applications and tools that educators can immediately use in classrooms for 21st-century readiness. Finally, in the Epilogue, we think together about how we can ensure the framework serves as a menu for equipping educators with equitable practices within the school and classroom. We chronicle a leader's experience in real-time as he navigates the complexities of ensuring educational equity in his school community.

SCENARIOS

We provide short anecdotes and scenarios to help others see themselves and their school situations within the complexities of ensuring educational equity in real time. They are composites of the teachers, principals, and others who have invited us into their learning spaces over the years. Their names and identifying characteristics were changed.

- **Stop and Reflect**—a set of reminders, situations, and reflections on how educators can use these practices in their own classrooms
- **Take Action**—a set of applications that teachers and instructional leaders can use and apply in their own classroom and school settings
- **Chapter Summary**—a set of major ideas from each chapter
- **Time to Dig In Tools**—a set of resources and tools for implementing educational equity

WHO IS THE BOOK FOR?

We wrote this book for two main audiences:

Classroom teachers: Most teachers are challenged by the recent disruptions in teaching and learning. The book provides teachers with resources, evidence-based strategies, and pedagogy to promote educational equity and address unfinished teaching and learning. In addition, we offer practical methods for connecting theory to on-the-ground teaching practices grounded in effective research-based practices. *Serving Educational Equity* is designed to support teachers' desire to address educational equity and student achievement as culturally responsive educators. An individual teacher can use the book as part of a professional learning community. This book is designed for educators, whether teachers, curriculum specialists, principals, or counselors. We are referring to all educators when using the term "teacher."

Instructional leaders and coaches: Instructional leaders and coaches are responsible for providing ongoing professional development, coaching, and instructional support in addressing the teacher challenges in real time. They are charged with delivering evidence-based, authentic practices and approaches to address unfinished teaching and learning issues. In addition, they serve as instructional experts who introduce teachers to quality resources, techniques, and methodology.

WHAT THIS BOOK IS AND WHAT IT IS NOT

This book is not a how-to guide with a prescriptive methodology; instead, it is written to provide multiple entry points to educators as they embark on a journey of equity and excellence for every child. The *Serving Educational Equity* frame is not a prescriptive program; it should instead be situated within the school or district context, allowing the data to speak to an educator's course of action to serve educational equity for instructional recovery.

The book embraces a mindset shift and a way of thinking that involves personal reflection on ensuring success for every child while removing biases and previous notions that could influence teaching. We agree with Barbara Blackburn (2020) that we must create learning environments that support rigor by ensuring that (a) each student is expected to learn at high levels, (b) each student is offered the support needed to achieve at high levels, and (c) each student actually demonstrates learning at high levels. As educators, we must provide classrooms where high expectations and the support needed for students to achieve at high levels should be offered to all children, no matter *their* ability level. Because low expectations turn into self-fulfilling prophecies of low academic performances, we must start with our mindsets and perceptions about the students we serve. For example, teachers who stigmatize certain students may modify how they teach, evaluate, and advise them, leading to poor educational outcomes for stigmatized students (Ferguson, 2003). Barbara Blackburn (2008) contends students believe in themselves when we, as teachers, believe in them. *Serving Educational Equity* offers organized tools, resources, and principles that provide a resource toolkit and menu of opportunities. Further, the text focuses on helping educators understand the principles that govern educating and stimulating students' abilities.

SUGGESTIONS FOR GETTING THE MOST OUT OF THE BOOK

- **Read with intention and purpose. Ask yourself guiding questions as you read.**
  How am I ensuring educational equity for all students? What do I want to know more about, or what questions or concerns do I have?

- **Read the book with a highlighter and a notebook.**
  As you read, determine the small nuggets of information for implementation. Make explicit connections to your current context and encourage conversations about mindset, bias, grade-level expectations, and scaffolding of learning. Utilize data team meetings to best meet the needs of students while making data decisions situational and responsive to students' socioemotional needs. Discuss ways to build lasting relationships with students that make them want to learn.

- **Customize tools and strategies.**
  Assess how you might adjust strategies and tools to fit your current context (grade level, school context, personality, and style).

- **Take bite-sized action.**
  Start small. Begin with one or two strategies to build relationships with students and colleagues. If you are beginning to explore educational equity, start with self-reflection techniques and address your own mindset about the students you serve. Think about your lived experiences and how they impact how you see your colleagues, students, and world. If you are a veteran of equitable best practices, focus on one or two areas to strengthen your practice.

- **Practice action research.**
  Utilize the *Strength-Weakness-Opportunities-Threat*s (SWOT) tool to construct guided questions and think about places to leverage the strengths and opportunities. Then, put your bite-sized actions into practice. Think about areas of growth and where threats could thwart your efforts. Understand that implementing equitable methods is cyclical and ongoing, and it creates space and time for interpretation. Finally, reflect and adjust your practices while keeping an open mind for new techniques and unique ways of thinking.

- **Invite others to join you on the journey.**
  Utilize opportunities and form book study groups to keep the conversation, accountability, and collaboration open within your school or district.

Take Action

In *The 7 Habits of Highly Effective People* (1990), author Stephen Covey distinguishes between proactive people who focus on what they can do and influence and reactive people who focus their energy on things beyond their control. The rationale for starting here is that many educational influences can make us feel overwhelmed, but we are more in control than we may think. We agree with Barbara Blackburn (2008) that we should focus on the things we can control and quit worrying about the things that are out of our control. As you savor parts of our book, take a moment to assess your mindset, which means examining the areas in which you have control and can take action. As educators embrace learning acceleration and educational equity, we should be reminded of our power and influence in the classroom.

Examine your mindset using Covey's Circle of Control diagram to determine your current mindset in addressing equity and learning acceleration (see Figure I.2).

Take a moment to ask yourself, "Do I have the power to make changes in my classroom?"

"Is this something I can decide to implement in my classroom?" (Blackburn, 2008, p. 2).

Figure I.2 • *Circle of Control and Influence*

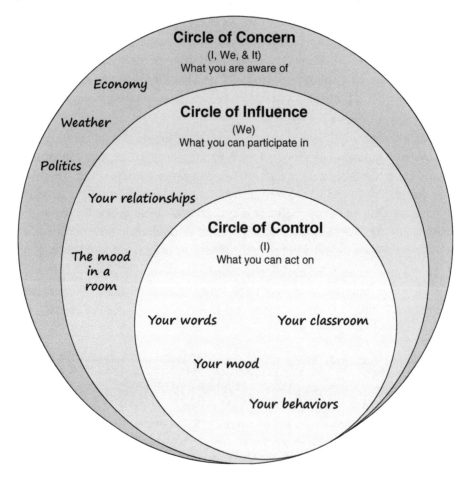

Source: Adapted from Covey (1990).

ACKNOWLEDGMENTS

Sonya

First, I would like to express my profound appreciation to my family. To my husband, Michael E. Darden; parents, Charles Murray Sr.; Shirley Murray, Leland Walton, brothers Charles Murray, Jr., Shaun Murray; sister Tonia Stringfellow, Marquita Monroe, aunt; Dorothy Monroe; uncle; Lauray & Darla Monroe and extended family, cousins, nieces, nephews, the Wades, Dardens, thank you for your unwavering support of my personal and professional endeavors.

Gwen, thank you for being a great friend. It has been an honor and privilege to write this book with you. Your attention to detail, profound storytelling, and overall brilliance helped to tell our story genuinely. Our vision for this book grew from our deep experience supporting educators as they navigate the complexities of an ever-changing world. I appreciate that we share an unapologetic vision that every child has the potential for excellence.

Dr. Linda Darling-Hammond, thank you for reading our book's early drafts and helping us reflect on how to use the science of learning for whole-child education. Your support on this journey has been invaluable. You are a true inspiration, and your research and passion for educational equity continue to shape education policy and practice worldwide.

Dr. Barbara Blackburn, thank you for being such an inspiration reminding us that rigor and relevance should be within reach for all students regardless of their zip code or ability level. Your wealth of knowledge on ways educators can ensure rigor and relevance for all permeates the pages of our book. Thank you for supporting our first book and then writing a beautiful foreword.

Thank you to my incredibly talented and compassionate Equity Matters family of consultants. And to all the leaders and teachers we work alongside, especially those educators within the Ohio, Missouri, Illinois, and Washington D.C. metropolitan areas, we honor you. Thank you for bravely sharing your stories. Your voices are woven into these pages. You make such a difference in the lives of students every day.

I want to give a special "shout out" to the schools and districts we support nationwide. Thank you, Education Plus, The Missouri Leadership Development System, and Achievement Network families, for all you do to support principals and the schools and communities they serve. Our students deserve an opportunity to have their talents, gifts, and skills celebrated, allowing them to thrive without boundaries. You help leaders realize that vision daily with your unwavering commitment to leader quality.

Dan Alpert and Megan Bedell, thank you for shepherding this book to the finish line as editors. You made the process manageable and attainable, giving excellent feedback and profound advice every step of the way. We appreciate your unswerving guidance and that of the entire Corwin team (Vijay, Natalie, Lucas, Melanie, Melissa, and Mia).

Gwen

A vision for this book emerged as we shared stories about the challenges teachers and students faced in this increasingly complex world. Throughout our careers, we have been committed to making a difference in the lives of children, and this book is our latest project to promote educational equity and assist educators in creating academic excellence for all learners.

Sonya, with your vision, dedication, and energy, we were able to see this dream become a reality. You are a true inspiration, and I want to thank you for being so dedicated to supporting teachers and advancing learning for children.

This project could only be completed with the support of family, friends, and our hard-working team at Corwin. I thank Megan, Dan, Natalie, Lucas, and Vijay for their never wavering guidance and support.

I, too, want to thank Dr. Linda Darling-Hammond for her early support of this initiative. She is truly a trailblazer in promoting educational equity.

Dr. Barbara Blackburn has been a guiding light through her work on rigor and learning. I appreciate her insight, dedication, and commitment to all students receiving rigorous instruction.

To my extended Turner family, I want to express my heartfelt appreciation for your continued encouragement and support for my professional and personal endeavors.

PUBLISHER'S ACKNOWLEDGMENTS

Corwin gratefully acknowledges the contributions of the following reviewers:

Jeff Austin
Principal
Social Justice Humanitas Academy
Los Angeles, CA

Ray Boyd
Principal
Dayton Primary School, Department of Education
Brabham, Australia

Janet Crews
Coordinator of Professional Learning
Clayton School District
Clayton, MO

Ken Darvall
School Principal
Tema International School
Tema, Ghana

Ronda Gray
Clinical Associate Professor in the School of Education
University of Illinois at Springfield
Springfield, Illinois

Rachael Lehr
Associate Principal
Dayton Primary School
Western Australia, Australia

Mitzi Mack
Teacher Librarian
Tampa, FL

Jacie Maslyk
Instructional Coach and Consultant
Pittsburgh, PA

Saundra Mouton
International Baccalaureate Primary Years Programme Coordinator, Reading
  Specialist, Assistant Principal, Global Schools Ambassador
Briarmeadow Charter School & Barbara Bush Elementary
Houston, TX

Cathy Patterson
Retired Elementary Educator/AP
Walnut Valley, USD
Walnut, CA

Lena Marie Rockwood
Assistant Principal for Student Success
Revere High School
Revere, MA

CHAPTER 1

SETTING THE TABLE FOR EQUITY AND EXCELLENCE

Planning for Student Equitable Success

> Every system is perfectly designed to get the results it gets.
> —W. Edwards Deming

Figure 1.1 • *Murray and Turner's (2021) Five-Course Framework for Accelerated Learning*

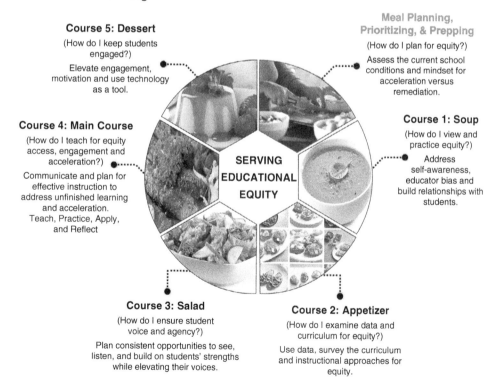

Course 5: Dessert
(How do I keep students engaged?)
Elevate engagement, motivation and use technology as a tool.

Meal Planning, Prioritizing, & Prepping
(How do I plan for equity?)
Assess the current school conditions and mindset for acceleration versus remediation.

Course 4: Main Course
(How do I teach for equity access, engagement and acceleration?)
Communicate and plan for effective instruction to address unfinished learning and acceleration.
Teach, Practice, Apply, and Reflect

SERVING EDUCATIONAL EQUITY

Course 1: Soup
(How do I view and practice equity?)
Address self-awareness, educator bias and build relationships with students.

Course 3: Salad
(How do I ensure student voice and agency?)
Plan consistent opportunities to see, listen, and build on students' strengths while elevating their voices.

Course 2: Appetizer
(How do I examine data and curriculum for equity?)
Use data, survey the curriculum and instructional approaches for equity.

CHAPTER ONE

- Discusses the importance of adult mindsets around approaches to acceleration versus remediation.

- Discusses why instructional advancement focuses on acceleration not remediation.

- Highlights the importance of assessing school climate and culture to design a menu that accelerates student learning.

- Discusses the Science of Learning and Development (*SoLD*) Principles in promoting equity.

- Outlines how educators can utilize the Strengths, Weaknesses, Opportunities, and Threats (SWOT) analysis tool to capture school data for accelerated learning and adaptive change.

ASSESS CURRENT CONDITIONS AND PLAN FOR SUCCESS

Planning for equitable learning is analogous to a chef's steps in meal planning. The chef selects the menu, prepares the ingredients, and plans for diners and the occasion. Educators also choose aligned curricula to prioritize learning, organize and internalize instruction, and plan for opportunities to advance student learning. This chapter allows us to embrace the Science of Learning and Development (*SoLD*) principle of acknowledging *Systems of Support* in which we meet student needs and address learning barriers by offering multi-tiered support systems. Also, we support the *SoLD* principle of creating *Social and Emotional Development*, which promotes the skills, habits, and mindsets that enable self-regulation, interpersonal skills, perseverance, and resilience as we engage in student-centered instruction. Finally, we embrace the *SoLD* principle of creating a *Supportive Environment* in which relational trust, a sense of safety, and belonging are addressed as structures for effective caring; see Figure 1.5. As we plan for students to engage in accelerated learning activities, we are reminded to explore and understand the current structures, systems, and students' academic needs. Throughout our work with teachers and students, we have realized that educators find the most academic success when they prepare for equitable instruction. In the following scenario of our Story From the Field, we present how teachers grappled with concerns and mindsets about their ability to recover learning for the students they serve.

Story From the Field #1

In a recent planning session with educators to review the new curriculum and discuss strategies for supporting student achievement, the following comments were overheard, "My students cannot do this work." "It is too hard." "How can I get them to grade-level work when they don't know their basic multiplication facts?" Another educator exclaimed, "I want to help them be successful, but they have too many gaps in their learning. Many of my twenty-five students cannot do grade-level work with a level of success. It makes me sad." These teachers returned to the old curriculum because it was easier for students to manage and comprehend.

The scenario above unfolded at one of many schools facing the dilemma of addressing learning loss. Conversations about how best to address student learning gaps have been discussed for years before the recent disruptions in teaching and learning. The educators in the above scenario expressed frustration, genuine concern, and anxiety about their student's abilities. Initially, these teachers sought to water down the learning by focusing on lower-level skills as the best option. Their response of offering students less challenging materials came from a sincere place, but were they loving *students to failure?* (Pearson, 2019). We support Barbara Blackburn's (2014) perspective that students can complete rigorous academic work at high levels when they receive the right support. Students are contending with learning gaps and emotional trauma, and caring adults may be inclined, in a subtle way, to lower the bar and protect students from challenging work. Our exchange made it apparent that an educator's mindset is critical to implementing change. We assert that it is essential to flip the script from *"What should I teach*?" to *"How do students learn*?" As there is a pivotal need to focus on student's potential rather than deficits, in the above Story From the Field, these educators wanted to help their students even if the assistance did not advance their learning. We believe that assisting educators like the ones in this scenario starts with helping them prioritize their instructional approach and strategies using planning that addresses unfinished learning. Barbara Blackburn (2008) suggests that educators set their vision for rigor and higher expectations by writing a planning letter. To embrace equity, we believe educators should articulate a clear plan that supports all students to reach their full academic potential. The letter should be specific and projected for the future and written a year from its date.

We believe the letter is a very effective strategy for addressing and changing the mindset for higher expectations for all students. When supporting teachers such as those in scenario one, we have embraced Zaretta Hammond's (2015) *Warm Demander* description, in which she characterizes teachers as *Warm Demanders*, *Elitists*, *Technocrats*, and *Sentimentalists*. Teachers and students have a learning partnership in which teachers are expected to guide students and offer support by not allowing students to engage in learned helplessness. See Chart 1.1. The stances indicate the nature of professional relationships between teachers and students as they engage with and instruct students. We support teachers who embrace and exhibit characteristics of the *Warm Demander* stance as they engage students in learning acceleration.

Warm Demanders explicitly:

1. Build rapport and trust
2. Show personal regard for students
3. Expect high expectations
4. Encourage productive struggle
5. Promote high standards
6. Scaffold learning to promote learner independence
7. Demonstrate respect and concern for students

In Chart 1.1, Zaretta Hammond provides the characteristics and roles of teachers as they engage with students. The stances are descriptions of the characteristics of teachers who exhibit some combination of professional distance (no focus or rapport) and passive leniency (no focus or effort) (Hammond, 2015).

Preparing to address unfinished teaching and learning requires educators to create conditions by understanding the teaching stances they are taking when determining the amount of cognitive load to provide. Zaretta Hammond's warm demander teaching stance offers an excellent tool for educators to self-reflect before executing teaching and learning.

How can we recognize the importance of both unfinished learning and unfinished teaching as critical focus areas to address student needs and their own role in advancing learning? UnboundEd Learning Inc. (2020) provides a profound definition of the two terms in Chart 1.2 on page 6.

Chart 1.1 • Warm Demander Chart

Active Demandingness

 THE WARM DEMANDER

- Explicit focus on building rapport and trust. Expresses warmth through non-verbal ways like smiling, touch, warm or firm tone of voice, and good natured teasing.
- Shows personal regard for students by inquiring about important people and events in their lives.
- Earns the right to demand engagement and effort.
- Very competent with the technical side of instruction.
- Holds high standards and offers emotional support and instructional scaffolding to dependent learners for reaching the standards.
- Encourages productive struggle.
- Viewed by students as caring because of personal regard and "tough love" stance.

THE TECHNOCRAT

- Has no explicit focus on building rapport. Doesn't focus on developing relationships with students, but does show enthusiasm for the subject matter.
- Holds high standards and expects students to meet them.
- Very competent with the technical side of instruction.
- Able to support independent learners better than dependent learners.
- Viewed by students as likeable even if distant because of teacher competence and enthusiasm for subject.

Personal Warmth ← | → **Professional Distance**

 THE SENTIMENTALIST

- Explicit focus on building rapport and trust. Expresses warmth through verbal and nonverbal communication.
- Shows personal regard for students.
- Makes excuses for students' lack of academic performance.
- Consciously holds lower expectations out of pity because of poverty or oppression. Tries to protect students from failure.
- Either over-scaffolds instruction or dumbs down the curriculum.
- Doesn't provide opportunities for students to engage in productive struggle.
- Allows students to engage in behavior that is not in their best interest.
- Liked by students but viewed as a push-over.

THE ELITIST

- No explicit or implicit focus on building rapport or trust.
- Keeps professional distance from students unlike himself.
- Unconsciously holds low expectations for dependent learners.
- Organizes instruction around independent learners and provides little scaffolding.
- Mistakes cultural differences of culturally and linguistically diverse students as intellectual deficits.
- Makes certain students feel pushed out of the intellectual life of the classroom.
- Allows dependent students to disengage from learning and engage in off-task behavior as long as not disruptive.
- Viewed by students as cold and uncaring.

Passive Leniency

Source: Hammond (2015, p. 17). Used with permission.

Chart 1.2 • *Unfinished Learning and Unfinished Teaching*

Unfinished Learning	Unfinished Teaching
"Grade level concepts and standards that students did not demonstrate proficiency in prior to entering the next grade" (UnboundEd Learning, Inc., 2020).	*"Grade level standards and concepts that were not directly taught nor assessed prior to students entering into the next grade"* (UnboundEd Learning, Inc., 2020).

Instructional Recovery starts with planning and a robust framework, such as the Science of Learning and Development (SoLD) Principles, to implement change. We believe that educators can move students to reach their full potential when they understand their current structures and systems along with their students' needs. Figure 1.2 outlines ways educators can address instructional recovery.

Figure 1.2 • *Where to Begin—Start With Planning*

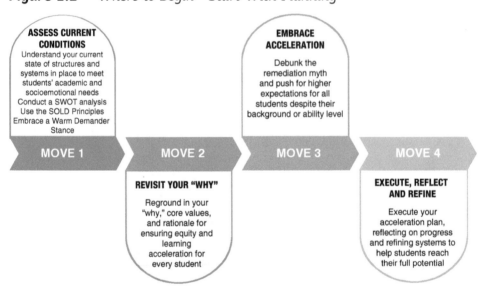

We start with an awareness of critical factors to enhance students' ability to reach their full potential. These factors include educator mindsets, students' abilities, instructional support, a positive learning environment, and opportunities for and evidence of mastery learning. Then, we flip the narrative from student learning loss to learning engagement. As educators are mired in thinking about how to recover student learning, the multitude of ways students can engage with successful grade-level work and tasks in meaningful ways can become buried in a sea of hopelessness about getting students back on track. Instead, the motivation and stamina for student learning can best be approached by recognizing the opportunities to address learning through our experiences. We have witnessed educators who share the following "why" statements as they strive to accelerate student learning:

- *I believe all students can achieve at high levels of instruction with access to grade-appropriate assignments, intense instruction, and high expectations.*
- *I believe students should be exposed to grade-level content regardless of their zip code, ability level, or background.*

Stop and Reflect

1. What is your *"why"* statement for student equity and excellence?

2. Do you believe all students should be provided access to grade-level content?

3. Do you have high expectations for all students when providing quality instructional experiences?

REVISIT YOUR PERSONAL *"WHY"*

We presented our personal *"why"* in the introduction of this book. For most schools, actual change starts with the educator's driving force or *"why"* (Sinek, 2009). The *"why"* serves as our purpose, cause, or belief that helps us carry out what we need to accomplish to make a change, and it has never been more critical today. If we, as educators, are going to make the transformational change required for instructional recovery for every child, our focus has to come from a deep place within us. The deep place is one that we hold sacred when the going gets tough. Educators who start with their *"why"* move to a place of realizing that student equity is more significant than their beliefs, perceptions, and thoughts about students' capabilities. Our *"why"* is more about ensuring students have a quality education that allows them to thrive as productive adults. Educators can embrace this idea by re-grounding and eradicating the biases they may hold about students and their capabilities. For example, an educator will want to embrace the idea that *all* students *can* learn and achieve while debunking the remediation myth.

Educators will want to push students forward academically and not continue in a cycle of failure that remediation has historically provided. *Just-in-time* versus

Just-in-case approaches to unfinished learning can shift mindsets and set the stage for quality teaching and learning. We offer explanations for the differences between the two approaches:

Shifting Adult Mindsets for Acceleration Versus Remediation Approaches

Just-in-time versus *Just-in-case* approaches:

Just-in-Case

A *Just-in-case* approach involves remediation that focuses on the strategies students failed to master in the previous year. It starts from a deficit mindset and pushes educators to focus on ways to recover the lost learning. *Just-in-case* scaffolding—providing hints and support to all students even when they have not demonstrated the need for it—creates issues of both access *and* equity (Dixon, 2020). *Just-in-case* approaches focus on the past and not students' present or future educational needs. In our experience, we have seen educators front-load math content making assumptions about what students still need to learn. Some will take a week to revisit below-level skills while elevating deficits based on their own beliefs about student capabilities. Teachers will also take time before a unit to review all the prerequisites they assume students did not master. These assumptions can sometimes be filled with misconceptions denying students access to grade-level content. We suggest instead an approach that uses real-time data that meets students where they are in the moment.

Just-in-Time

A *Just-in*-time approach pushes the mindset that we can help students where they are and get them where we want them by filling in the gaps and keeping the focus on high expectations. The focus is on the student's present and future learning needs. We agree with The National Council of Teachers of Mathematics (2018) that a *Just-in-time* approach is required to advance student learning. A suggested method is to give students an exit ticket at the end of the preceding lesson, testing the next lesson's prerequisites.

The NCTM council (2018) advises:

> **Teachers should connect prerequisite skills to grade level or concise level content to deepen students' mathematical understanding. Regardless of what has**

come before, on-grade-level mathematics content must
be the focus of our work with students.

We discuss this idea more in Chapter 5 with in-depth approaches and
suggestions, including sample lesson plans. Moreover, to reimagine teaching and
learning, we need to focus on acceleration, not remediation. Chart 1.3 offers
clear guidance on the differences between acceleration and remediation
approaches (Figure 1.3).

*Chart 1.3 • Suzy Pepper-Rollins (2014) Acceleration and
Remediation: A Comparison*

	Acceleration	Remediation
Self-efficacy	• Self-confidence and engagement increase. • Academic progress is evident.	• Students perceive they're in the "slow class," and self-confidence and engagement decrease. • Backward movement leads to a sense of futility and lack of progress.
Basic skills	• Skills are hand-picked just in time for new concepts. • Students apply skills immediately.	• Instruction attempts to reteach every missing skill. • Skills are taught in isolation and not applied to current learning.
Prior knowledge	• Critical prior knowledge is provided ahead of time, enabling students to connect to new information.	• Prior knowledge is not connected to new learning.
Relevance	• Treats relevance as a critical component of student motivation and memory.	• Relevance is not seen as a priority.
Connection to core class	• Instruction is connected to core class; ongoing collaboration is emphasized.	• Instruction is typically isolated from the core class.

(Continued)

(Continued)

	Acceleration	Remediation
Pacing and direction	• Active, fast-paced, hands-on. • Forward movement; goal is for students to learn on time with peers.	• Passive, with a focus on worksheets or basic software programs. • Backward movement; the goal is for students to "catch up" to peers.

Source: Rollins (2014). Used with permission by ASCD.

Figure 1.3 • *Remediation Versus Acceleration*

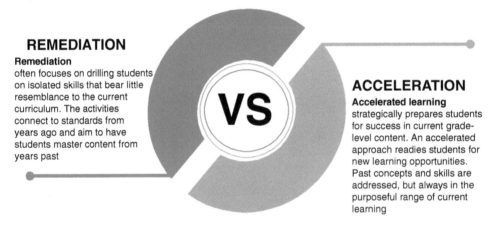

REMEDIATION

Remediation
often focuses on drilling students on isolated skills that bear little resemblance to the current curriculum. The activities connect to standards from years ago and aim to have students master content from years past

ACCELERATION

Accelerated learning
strategically prepares students for success in current grade-level content. An accelerated approach readies students for new learning opportunities. Past concepts and skills are addressed, but always in the purposeful range of current learning

Source: Adapted from TNTP (2020) and Learning in the Fast Lane (Pepper-Rollins, 2014).

Stop and Reflect

1. How do you currently address unfinished teaching and learning?

2. What resonates with you from the *"just-in-time"* or *"just-in-case"* instructional approaches to instructional recovery?

EMBRACE ACCELERATION!

Instructional Advancement Through Acceleration Versus Remediation

We suggest that educators devote the bulk of classroom time to acceleration, challenging instruction at grade level or higher, and giving all students "the good stuff": a rich, high-quality curriculum in English language arts, mathematics, social studies, science, and the arts as outlined in the Acceleration Imperative (Thomas Fordham Institute, 2021). The idea of acceleration for learning gain is not new; Suzy Pepper-Rollins (2014) showcases the difference between acceleration and remediation in Chart 1.3. However, we believe acceleration is at the core of planning equitable instruction for *all* students. A new lens for educational equity can be achieved after providing access and opportunity for students regardless of zip codes or backgrounds.

Stop and Reflect

1. What resonates after reviewing the Acceleration versus Remediation chart?

2. Are you implementing acceleration or remediation in your current instructional practices?

3. How could you use ideas from the chart to implement more acceleration practices in your school or classroom?

Debunking the Remediation Myth

A common theme of the teachers' comments in Story From the Field #1 embraced remediation as a best practice. Statements such as "*Students cannot move on if they don't know basic facts*" and "*None of my students can do grade-level work due to learning gaps*" indicate that we are utilizing an approach that embraces remediation. Acceleration takes the direction that we move forward and connect the new learning to the core instruction and what is occurring in the classroom now. Students of color and those from low-income backgrounds were more likely than their white, wealthier peers to experience remediation—even when they had already demonstrated success on grade-level content. Learning acceleration was particularly effective for students of color and those from low-income families (TNTP, 2021; ZEARN, 2021).

This is strong evidence that learning acceleration works and could be critical to unwinding generations-old academic inequities the COVID-19 pandemic has only exacerbated. The remediation myth indicates that teachers can best support students by meeting them at their performance level and focusing on past failures. Educators have embraced this long-standing perception as the most effective strategy for improving student learning. However, children who are behind stay behind when remediation is the focus (UNESCO, 2020). The remediation myth, meeting students at their performance level rather than their potential level, has been a well-practiced approach to student-learning recovery. In actuality, *"meeting students where they are practically guarantees they will lose more academic ground and get even less access to grade-level work in the future"* (Czupryk, 2020). If educators embark upon instructional recovery, they will want to debunk this myth and develop an understanding of support for all students having grade-level access to learning recovery.

In our experience, we have witnessed marginalized students impacted mainly by these remediation approaches. The groups most vulnerable are children of color, children from low-income families, children with special needs, and students learning English (Steiner & Weisberg, 2020). Amy Takabori of Carnegie Learning (2021) reminds us that remediation *is entrenched in the past: what students missed last year and what they need to redo. On the other hand, acceleration focuses on the present: what students need right now to excel this year.*

In the groundbreaking report *Accelerate, Don't Remediate* (TNTP, 2021; ZEARN, 2021) the authors suggest that "students who experienced learning acceleration struggled less and learned more than students who started at the same level but experienced remediation instead. Students of color and those from low-income backgrounds were more likely than their white, wealthier peers to experience remediation—even when they had already demonstrated success on grade-level content. Learning acceleration was particularly effective for students of color and those from low-income families" (p. 4). The New Teacher Project (TNTP) (2018) study showed that giving students watered-down content practically guarantees they will lose more academic ground. The major findings of this research revealed that students failed to be provided grade-appropriate assignments, strong instruction, deep engagement, and high expectations. We pondered how students actually engaged in meaningful learning at their grade level. According to the TNTP study (2018), out of the estimated 180 hours of instruction per subject area, students only spent approximately 47 hours on meaningful engagement at grade level (Figure 1.4). We need to engage students in authentic and meaningful learning experiences, not just engage them in meaningless practices that do not advance learning.

Figure 1.4 • *Hours of Meaningful Grade Level Engagement*

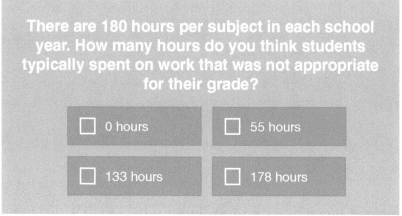

Students spent 133 hours on work that was not appropriate for their grade.

School Disruptions, Learning Loss, and Remediation

The unprecedented interruptions in schooling due to COVID-19 and other factors have exposed equity gaps in learning. As a result of natural disasters, pandemics, family displacements, school closings, and remote learning, students have experienced depression, anxiety, behavioral problems, and posttraumatic stress disorders (DiMenna, 2021; Salciccioli, 2021; Weems et al., 2010). One example was the devastation of schools after Hurricane Katrina in New Orleans. Educators who sought to address the learning needs of students after the Katrina hurricane disaster discovered that students who were offered traditional remedial education in New Orleans schools continued to suffer learning losses. Paul (2020) reports that New Orleans schools focused on remediation resulting in students who scored so badly on their end-of-school-year standardized assessments that their schools faced closures. Consequently, when these schools changed their instructional focus to grade-level instruction, the students improved their academic performances. This was further evidence that remediation could lock students in a vicious cycle of failure. After Katrina, many educators regrouped and moved students to typical grade-level classes and taught "*just-in-time*" instruction to address this problem (DiMenna, 2021; Gonser, 2020; Paul, 2020). We embrace this philosophy and methodology, encouraging educators to take advantage of opportunities to provide students with grade-level content even if the students are performing below grade level academically. Throughout our experiences, we have learned that school disruptions can lead to significant learning losses, and this is the crucial time to focus on acceleration, not remediation, to advance learning.

Stop and Reflect

How can we use the instructional recovery efforts of educators after Hurricane Katrina to inform our approach to accelerated learning that addresses unfinished learning and teaching?

DESIGNING THE MENU FOR STUDENT SUCCESS

Learning recovery, unfinished teaching, and unfinished learning are critical topics for conversation to help educators think about how students learn. Due to interruptions, there are gaps in what educators teach and what students have not mastered.

A chef's meal-planning steps are analogous to student learning planning. The practical steps of meal planning involve selecting recipes, choosing ingredients, and preparing meals. Educators can use a similar process to ensure equitable student practices. They can plan for meaningful instruction by utilizing data to ensure engaging practices are responsive to the needs of the students they serve. Reflecting on the organization's purpose and using the school's curriculum can provide excellent guides and road maps for planning, with educators utilizing effective techniques (or ingredients) to accelerate student learning. Prioritizing instructional support allows educators to address unfinished learning as they qualitatively and quantitatively evaluate their current climate and respond to student needs.

Science of Learning and Development Principles

At this point in your reading, you may be asking about the best approach to take in supporting your students' instructional recovery. We contend that the *Science of Learning and Development Principles* (*SoLD*) (Darling-Hammond et al., 2020) (Figure 1.5) can serve as the basis and foundation to help schools address

Figure 1.5 • *Science of Learning and Development Principles (SoLD)*

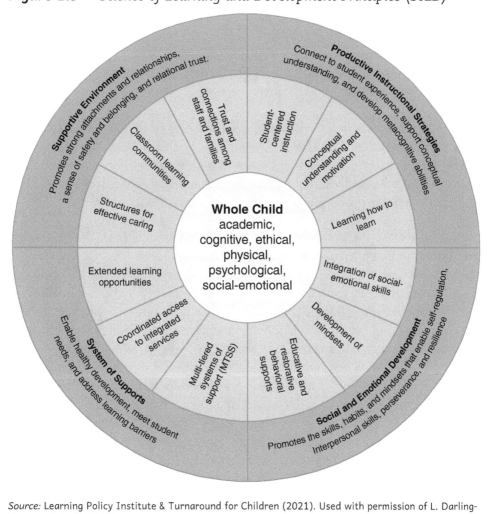

Source: Learning Policy Institute & Turnaround for Children (2021). Used with permission of L. Darling-Hammond et al. (2021).

today's acute need for a new kind of educational system optimized for student learning, recovery, and development.

The *SoLD* principles help educators recognize the need for whole child development in the education program (Figure 1.5). Five key elements are used as guiding principles for promoting equity: (a) positive developmental relationships, (b) environments filled with safety and belonging, (c) rich learning experiences and knowledge development, (d) development of positive skills, habits, and mindsets, and (e) integrated support systems (Darling-Hammond et al., 2020; Learning Policy Institute & Turnaround for Children, 2021). The

SoLD principles include evidence-based strategies that help students connect to their experiences, promote conceptual understanding, and improve their metacognitive abilities.

THE SWOT ANALYSIS: AN ADAPTIVE CHANGE TOOL

We support teachers in addressing student learning needs by first assessing their current realities with the *SoLD* principles and their "why" as guides for answering the questions, "*How am I serving all the needs of my students? Do I have a whole child approach?*" We suggest educators engage in the SWOT analysis to answer those questions (Piercy & Giles, 1989).

Strengths are the factors that we control, do well, and access. Weaknesses are factors within our control that detract from our ability to accelerate student learning. Opportunities are resources and trends available. Finally, threats are the areas we have no control over but can benefit by having contingency plans to address them if they should occur (Madsen, 2016). In any organization, especially our schools and classrooms, it is pivotal to understand the current state before testing or implementing changes. The SWOT analysis could help educators set the stage for improved learning. A SWOT analysis could be utilized to assess data-informed teaching and learning conditions that situate instructional recovery and educational equity. Exploring what is working, what threats exist, what needs improvement, and how resources may influence those improvements, opportunities, and practices allowed the educators in Story From the Field #1 to change how they structured the learning outcomes of their students. The SWOT analysis could help educators set the stage for improved learning. See the Time to Dig in Tools for a link to a blank SWOT analysis.

Execute, Reflect, and Refine

Activity 1.1 SWOT Analysis

SWOT: Use the chart to assess your current school or classroom conditions. Once you have analyzed your current situation, plan to take action on your findings.

Before we engage in educational equity for acceleration, we need to understand our current reality. The SWOT activity should be completed to understand the internal

(Continued)

and external factors affecting classroom instruction and student learning. Consider the following questions.

Teachers:

- Strengths: What strengths do you have in meeting students' needs? How do you successfully accelerate students' learning?
- Weakness: Where would you like to improve your efforts to help all students find success?
- Opportunities: What opportunities do you have to make accelerated student learning a reality in your classroom?
- Threats: What threats compromise your ability to support all students?

Instructional Leaders/Coaches:

- Strengths: What strengths do you have in your building as related to instructional recovery and student engagement?
- Weakness: Where would you like to improve your efforts to help all teachers and students in your building find success?
- Opportunities: What opportunities do you have to accelerate student learning in your building?
- Threats: What threats compromise your ability to support all students in your building?

SWOT: Use the chart below to assess your current school or classroom conditions. Once you have analyzed your current situation, plan to take action on your findings.

Chart 1.4 • Strengths, Weaknesses, Opportunities, and Threats (SWOT) Analysis

Strengths	Weaknesses
What strengths do I have in meeting students' needs? How do I successfully accelerate students' learning? In what ways do I provide equitable instruction for my students?	Where would I like to improve my efforts to help all students find success?

(Continued)

(Continued)

Opportunities	Threats
What opportunities are open to accelerate student learning? What trends/resources could I take advantage of as I consider the educational equity needs of my students? How can my students benefit from those opportunities?	What factors are potential threats? Threats include factors beyond my control that could risk helping students meet their goals. What contingency plan can I put in place should these threats occur?

Source: © 2021, Adapted by Sonya Murray for Equity Matters. All rights reserved.

Once you have completed the SWOT analysis, explore your answers to the following guided questions:

Guided Questions

- How are you planning for whole child development?
- How can you reflect on strengths and opportunities from the SWOT analysis?
- How can you reflect on weaknesses and threats from the SWOT analysis?
- How are you embracing and building on strengths while reducing the weaknesses and threats?
- How can data be utilized to inform students' academic abilities?
- How are students practicing and applying what they learn in meaningful ways?

Setting the Table After the SWOT Analysis

Educators must intentionally address inequality and the status quo in classroom practices, school policies, and instructional activities. After conducting a SWOT analysis, it is reasonable to reflect on moving forward. After conducting strategic planning that moves all students forward academically, we recommend that educators establish their own personal "why" prioritizing those key elements that focus on learning acceleration. The SWOT analysis can be used as educators establish their own personal "why" prioritizing key elements that focus on acceleration and learning gain.

Prioritizing Key Elements

Reflecting on students' learning outcomes, exploring "*why*" practices and values, and examining data used to inform instruction allow educators to embrace prerequisites for equity. A critical step in planning for equity includes the activities identified in Chart 1.5.

Chart 1.5 • Prioritizing the Menu for Educational Equity

_____ Engage in a SWOT analysis of best practices that ensure educational equity and student acceleration.

_____ Revisit your "*why*" as a driving force and the school's mission, vision, and core values around remediation versus accelerated approaches.

_____ Stamp your "*why*" with equitable actions around acceleration, and reimagination of teaching and learning.

_____ Understand your own mental models, perceptions, and biases to clearly see your students free of preconceived notions and self-fulfilling prophecies.

_____ Determine barriers to educational equity with students that embrace empathy and deep appreciation for their cultural differences and diverse needs.

Stop and Reflect

Reflect on the items in the *Prioritizing the Menu for Educational Equity* checklist as you prepare to set the table for acceleration and instructional recovery.

Educator's Response in Story From the Field #1

The educators in Story From the Field #1 ran a SWOT analysis and, after the deeper data analysis, determined that more students were successful with grade-level content than they initially thought. They used the information to inform instruction. They determined that implicit biases and perceptions often overshadowed data or information revealed to educators during data analysis. Further, data analysis revealed accurate gaps in student learning, yet the weaknesses were not as glaring as they initially thought. Teachers reflected on their opportunities to address student misconceptions and used data to drive instruction. The teachers discovered that intermittent schooling and student attendance were mitigating factors that posed problems, and they became more flexible in providing students access to assignments. The SWOT analysis allowed these educators to assess the present state of teaching and learning without preconceived biases about the students' abilities.

Educators were encouraged to assess their current conditions in response to their questions from Story From the Field #1. The SWOT offered a great starting point for discussions on what worked and why in their classrooms. The educators in Story From the Field #1 reported that looking at the SWOT data independently and then as a collaborative team provided more cohesion, focus, and purpose as they prepared for accelerated learning. A critical action after the SWOT would require educators to examine their own beliefs, values, and practices. Instead of just focusing on the learning deficits of their students, they explored learning potential, possibilities, and techniques. They needed to examine their own philosophical beliefs about student capabilities. As a result, they believed they were better prepared to meet their students' academic needs. After gaining an honest appraisal of current conditions, it was time for these educators to look inwardly at motivating factors. These motivating factors drive us and constitute our "*why*" and the reasons we engage in the vital work of educational equity. This crucial analysis step for planning allowed these teachers to prioritize their actions.

Principal Jacob's School

Another school leader in the Midwest, Principal Jacob, who we support, implemented a SWOT analysis to identify critical actions in response to acceleration. He implemented the SWOT analysis with his staff to better understand areas that the staff could leverage in helping students reach their full potential. He used the SWOT to determine the best initiatives for acceleration and student engagement to be implemented with his teachers and staff. It was an eye-opening experience for him and supported his vision of becoming transparent about strategic planning at his school, especially in acceleration. The SWOT analysis allowed strategic planning to occur at various levels, opening the opportunity for transparency, collegiality, and the diverse perspectives of staff and students. As a school leader, he captured and identified three emerging themes: (1) *Staff Relationship*s could be enhanced by team building, sharing best practices, and empathy for collegiality and trust. (2) *Student Voice*s could be elevated more at the school to ensure more robust engagement. (3) *Instructional Practice* could be enhanced by acceleration and equitable practices. The school reflected on opportunities to garner more parent support to meet acceleration approaches to maximize students' learning. We conclude our book with more information on how Principal Jacob's school consistently worked to elevate educational equity through acceleration in our Epilogue.

Take Action

Now that you have explored prepping, prioritizing, and planning for educational equity, act on your learning by completing the following application.

Read, Respond, and Reflect

Read Story From the Field #1 again and think about other comments by educators:

- *"We must teach many standards, knowing the students will struggle academically."*
- *"It is overwhelming, and I cannot begin to focus on one or two standards when students need attention, and there are holes in their learning from prior years."*
- *"I need to go back and teach students what they missed because how will they learn the grade-level content when they missed prerequisites from previous years?"*

Let's Reflect

- What are your reactions to the quotes above? Do you agree or disagree?
- Have you assessed strengths, weaknesses, and opportunities for acceleration and instructional recovery?
- What would your SWOT analysis reveal about your current conditions?
- How has the push for learning recovery impacted your teaching and learning?

Respond

- How do you plan for students' access to grade-level instruction who have significant gaps in their learning?
- Do you believe all your students can achieve at high academic levels? Why or Why not?

SUMMARY

As evident throughout this chapter, educators must plan for student success; it does not happen without active engagement. Achieving equity in education is a multifaceted planning process using deliberate actions and personal reflection. Equity does not just happen; it involves planning so that every student receives what is needed for academic potential, cognition, and social development. We believe the planning must be systematic and grounded in a theoretical framework such as the SoLD principles. Students who have experienced learning loss and, or are not performing at grade level need support that accelerates their learning. The research does not support the continued use of remediation but rather a focus on acceleration to address learning loss. As we embrace acceleration for learning, we push for higher expectations for all students regardless of their backgrounds and ability levels. Educators who want to help students achieve their academic potential can begin with a SWOT analysis while embracing equity by exploring their values, beliefs, and current instructional practices. They can explore their own "why" as they make decisions that impact learning acceleration. Achieving equity for students, who have been marginalized, requires an honest exploration of data, an examination of instructional methods, a review of learning environments and relationships, and then taking actions that move students forward. We offer a road map in Chapter 2 to help educators embrace self-awareness and a whole-child focus while creating a rapport with each child.

 **TIME TO DIG IN TOOLS**

These provide additional resources for enhancing equity and accelerating learning.

Activity	Description	Research Support and Reference	Link
Strengths, Weaknesses, Opportunities, Threats (SWOT)	An essential tool for administration, teachers, and staff to identify practical and less effective elements in your school and can be utilized to plan strategies for achieving student achievement goals.	The origin of the term "SWOT" is unknown. SWOT analysis was described by Learned, E. P., Christensen, C. R., & Andrews, K. R. (1969). Business policy: Text and cases. RD Irwin. The tool was adapted for school educators to use for assessing their school climate and culture.	https://qrs.ly/bxeqdvs
The Acceleration Imperative	*The Acceleration Imperative*, an open-source, evidence-based document created with input from dozens of current and former chief academic officers, scholars, and others with deep expertise and experience in high-performing, high-poverty elementary schools.	Davidson, B., & Woodward, G. (March 2021). *The Acceleration Imperative. A plan to address elementary students' unfinished learning in the wake of COVID-19.* Thomas B. Fordham Institute. https://eric.ed.gov/?id=ED613178	https://www.CAOCentral.org
Warm Demander Chart	The stances are descriptions of the characteristics of teachers who exhibit some combination of	Zaretta Hammond, 2019. All rights reserved. www.CRTandthe Brain.com	https://qrs.ly/d3eqdw9

(Continued)

(Continued)

Activity	Description	Research Support and Reference	Link
	professional distance (no focus or rapport) and passive leniency (no focus or effort) (Hammond, 2015).		
SoLD Principles	Developmental systems' framework that supports well-vetted learning strategies, learning opportunities, and relationships needed to promote children's well-being and learning.	Learning Policy Institute & Turnaround for Children. (2021). *Design principles for schools: Putting the science of learning and development into action.*	https://qrs.ly/ soeqdwh
Rigor in Your Classroom: A Toolkit for Teachers	This book contains a wealth of free resources that can be downloaded for the classroom to increase rigor and relevance in teaching and learning.	Blackburn, B. (2014). *Rigor in your classroom: A toolkit for teachers.* Routledge.	https://qrs.ly/ v6eqdys

CHAPTER 2

SOUP FOR THE SOUL

Building Equity Literacy and
Solid Relationships for Whole Child Development

> No significant learning can occur without a
> significant relationship.
> —James Comer

Figure 2.1 • *Murray and Turner's (2021) Five-Course Framework for Accelerated Learning*

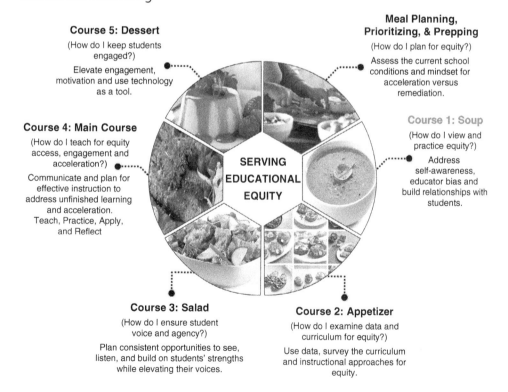

Course 5: Dessert
(How do I keep students engaged?)
Elevate engagement, motivation and use technology as a tool.

Meal Planning, Prioritizing, & Prepping
(How do I plan for equity?)
Assess the current school conditions and mindset for acceleration versus remediation.

Course 4: Main Course
(How do I teach for equity access, engagement and acceleration?)
Communicate and plan for effective instruction to address unfinished learning and acceleration. Teach, Practice, Apply, and Reflect

SERVING EDUCATIONAL EQUITY

Course 1: Soup
(How do I view and practice equity?)
Address self-awareness, educator bias and build relationships with students.

Course 3: Salad
(How do I ensure student voice and agency?)
Plan consistent opportunities to see, listen, and build on students' strengths while elevating their voices.

Course 2: Appetizer
(How do I examine data and curriculum for equity?)
Use data, survey the curriculum and instructional approaches for equity.

CHAPTER TWO

- Introduces the impact of equity literacy, compassion, and socioemotional learning using the *SoLD* Principles for learning acceleration.
- Explains the teacher–student relationship connection for whole child development and learning acceleration, analogous to soup to a meal.
- Highlights the importance of recognizing and respecting diverse backgrounds.

We use a muti-course meal analogy in providing our research-based framework for building equity and accelerating learning; see Figure 2.1. This stage of our multistep process is sustenance to the learning process, like *soup* is to the meal. Soup is usually fulfilling, healing, and enriching. We support positive educator/ student relationships which focus on their belonging and the importance of creating mutually respectful environments. Students will likely respond positively to equity-literate educators who invest in their success. Relationships where teachers care about students' success and show empathy can be used as critical strengthening agents to motivate students and advance their learning. This chapter allows us to embrace the *SoLD* principle of creating a *Supportive Environment* in which relational trust, a sense of safety, and belonging are addressed as structures for effective caring. This trust includes teachers, students, and families. A supportive environment reduces anxiety and enables learning. Building relationships should be the cornerstone for learning, as the Learning Policy Institute (2021) reminds us that "the brain is always developing as a product of relationships and experiences." Zaretta Hammond (2015) asserts, "It is imperative to understand how to build positive social relationships that signal to the brain a sense of physical, psychological, and social safety so that learning is possible."

Story From the Field #2
Sonya's Story

    As a new administrator in the building, I got to know my staff, colleagues, and students. As is customary in a new situation, I intended to quickly get to know all the students in my care. Our staff eagerly shared insights about many students, including Mark Doe (pseudonym). Mark, a seventh grader was the subject of many staff comments because of his disciplinary record. All descriptions of him addressed his incomplete assignments and inappropriate behavior. Mark was accustomed to negative interactions and experiences with several students and staff at the school. He told me he was failing, had a discipline record, and hated school when we first met. Because I knew the importance of establishing a positive working relationship with every child, I informed him that I was excited to meet him and looked forward to a great working relationship. However, he was skeptical and disclosed tremendous personal and home struggles. He informed me that no one cared for him except an aunt, whom he knew loved him, but grew weary of his constant school issues. Mark's behavior was part of a self-fulfilling prophecy: of "the adults expect inappropriate behavior; therefore, the child misbehaves." Children will become what you say they are (Blease, 1983; Palardy, 1969).

As the lead administrator, it was my responsibility to help my staff successfully connect and engage Mark and others like him. The teachers and I explored our behaviors and actions to reach Mark. Our first effort was to engage Mark in meaningful and supportive experiences. His teachers were asked to examine *how* they provided guidance, communicated with him, and engaged him in learning activities. We helped him create a joint plan of action and schedule to work on assignments; he needed to improve his learning tools. Breaking this cycle of failure was not always easy, but it certainly is possible. Changes in mindset for both teachers and students have to occur.

Mark's preparation and participation in an essay contest (A Dream for the Future) for middle school students was a significant turning point. When I first introduced the idea, Mark responded, "I cannot write, and besides, my discipline record is too bad? Nobody will read it." I responded, "I will read it and believe in you." He initially told me he was not interested and stated his inability; but later, he asked me about the essay and began crafting a draft. We established a plan, and each day, working on the paper became his center of focus. A few other teachers participated in the writing process; these teachers were surprised by his writing ability and newfound interest. There were challenges and setbacks, but Mark had begun to trust the adults and himself. He became a better writer and a better student because of the positive relationships with the small cadre of adults who demonstrated commitment to his success. Mark completed his essay and was selected as one of the three finalists. As a finalist, he was asked to wear a yellow scarf, signifying his status as a winner. The color yellow symbolizes optimism, confidence, creativity, and emotional strength (Wright, 1998). Indeed, Mark shared a newfound sense of confidence, commitment, and determination that had not previously existed. His teachers connected the essay celebration to his ability to make better choices, and he did. Teachers started seeing his potential, not his past failures. His aunt shared her gratitude and appreciation for changing his trajectory. Mark's story and many others solidify how underlying messages relating to expectations, perceptions, and subsequent actions could allow or deny students access to future success.

In Story From the Field #2, Mark's experience chronicled those of students across the country whose behavior overshadowed their academic ability, drowned by the perceptions and biases of others (Hannigan & Hannigan, 2016). Mark's teachers realized that their initial actions, behaviors, and beliefs had not supported or provided him with the tools necessary for academic success. The experiences with Mark allowed everyone to reflect on how our practices helped or hindered student success. We know it can be difficult to connect with challenging students, but the success and the result will be worth it. Teaching students how to manage their social skills leads to tremendous academic success. Children with high social skills are four times as likely to graduate from college (Bornstein, 2015). Psychologist Abraham Maslow (1943) has shown through his research that unless basic human needs are met (security, housing, nutrition), it is difficult for children to develop and grow up to be healthy, well-adjusted adults.

Story From the Field #3
Sonya's Story

As an administrator in a high-poverty school district of over a thousand students, I remember collaborating with my staff on opportunities to break down potential barriers to student success. As a staff, we brainstormed strategies that could better help us address the hierarchy of students' needs. We recognized our approach would need to be strategic and out-of-the-box, as financial resources were limited. Creating a culture of empathy coupled with high expectations and mutual respect would require us to "see" students, as well as invest in their well-being at school and home. Our primary goal was to help students find academic success by removing barriers that prevented them from reaching their full potential. After initially trying to meet the vast needs of our students using our school-level and personal resources, we quickly realized the unrealistic demands of that approach. We needed to invest our community in this endeavor and explore the possibilities of engaging in several partnerships. Some partnerships, such as our school/university collaborations, provided a win-win situation in which our students teamed with Gwen's university tutors to share learning experiences. We extended our collaborations by inviting external community members to support us in ways they felt comfortable. Our "coffee and conversation" meetings with constituents about ways to help our school were transformational. We were surprised to see the many ways our community constituents wanted to invest, but they were unsure how to get involved. Elevating their ideas led to a mindset shift. We saw the community, parents, and partners as the fabric of our student's success. We partnered with local foundations that helped us meet students' wrap-around needs like uniform and clothing support, medical attention, shelter outreach, and food access. Our efforts were highly successful and led to other endeavors such as student-published books, on-campus medical aid and mental health resources, guitars and music lessons, which led to our first guitar concerts, academic tutoring, and resources for students, a donated science garden, partnerships with local universities, a donated newly furnished science lab, and an on-site parent resource hub. Our students engaged in on-site and virtual tutoring with a local university and received complimentary tickets and transportation to sports arenas.

We were creating a "whole child" approach to teaching and learning. Our school environment became more inviting, welcoming, and supportive and one where educators/students/and parents felt like they belonged. Our primary goal was to build empathy and understanding for our students, but this new way of operating gave us much more. We learned that advancing students' academic knowledge required us to understand them and their environment holistically. When we tapped into students' interests and built solid relationships, students felt valued and supported beyond the school's four walls, which led to educational equity and maximized success. Our students could explore a world beyond their neighborhood, and our partners and community constituents engaged in helping our students reach their full potential. The mindset shift occurred when school personnel was able to receive support from the greater community, who demonstrated their care and concern for the future of our children.

Through Story From the Field #3, we were privileged to see how important it is to meet not only students' academic needs but also their personal, emotional, and social needs. By engaging with parents and community partners, one school opened up a world beyond the classroom for its students and helped to create a mindset shift. This shift occurred with the school personnel, who realized that others care about children and their success. A mindset shift occurred with many of the community partners, who never realized the potential of many children in high-poverty schools.

We encourage educators to examine the Learning Policy Institute's *Guiding Principles for Equitable Whole-Child Design* (2021), Figure 2.2 which concludes that if the right conditions for learning are used, students will not only learn, but they will thrive. The right conditions include positive relationships, integrated support systems, rich learning experiences, and culturally affirming practices within a safe environment. These guiding principles have been embraced throughout our book. We support the development for the *whole child. Research suggests that whole child development, not routine or standardized classroom-based learning, empowers children as creative and engaged citizens who can strengthen the well-being of a whole society* (Thomsen & Ackermann, 2015, p. 1). We embrace The Learning Policy Institute's (2021) *Essential Guiding Principles for Whole-Child Design, which allow educators to implement the SoLD principles.*

We encourage educators to examine the Learning Policy Institute's Guiding Principles for Equitable Whole-Child Design (2021) (Figure 2.2), which concludes that if the right conditions for learning are used, students will not only learn, but they will thrive. The right conditions include positive relationships, integrated support systems, rich learning experiences, and culturally affirming practices within a safe environment. These guiding principles have been embraced throughout our book.

Figure 2.2 • *Essential Guiding Principles for Equitable Whole-Child Design*

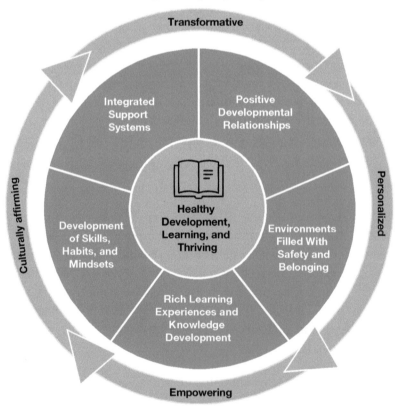

Source: Learning Policy Institute & Turnaround for Children (2021). Used with permission of L. Darling-Hammond et al. (2021).

Figure 2.3 • *Where to Begin? Building Equity Literacy, Trauma Awareness for Student Belonging*

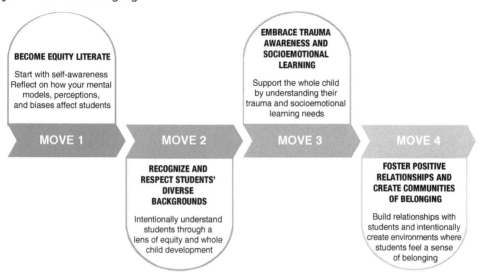

So how should we begin setting students up for social and emotional success in order to attain learning acceleration? This chapter highlights how educators can unlock the learning potential of all students they serve; see Figure 2.3. This stage of our multistep process supports and enhances the learning process, like **soup** to a meal. First, we make the case that educators must build equity literacy to form relationships that develop the whole child for accelerated teaching and learning.

BECOMING EQUITY LITERATE

We make the claim that educators can best build relationships by becoming equity literate. Equity literate educators:

1. understand that their perceptions and biases impact the students they serve,
2. reflect on their expectations and stay abreast of factors that affect students, and
3. cultivate and sustain bias-free and discrimination-free learning communities. (Equity Literacy Institute, 2021)

> The focus on equity literacy requires an understanding that doing so is a primary responsibility of everyone in civil society.
> —Gorski (2013)

Taking the time to examine one's perceptions is the first step in self-exploration and can lead to a mindset shift about students and their abilities. If you cannot see students without preconceived notions, you will not push them beyond your expectations. Therefore, we claim that educators need to support students by examining their expectations, perceptions, and beliefs. As we think about addressing, unpacking, and understanding the uniqueness of students while examining our perceptions of their abilities, we can value or devalue their potential opportunities. Mark's example reminds us that teachers must be honest in their self-appraisal about their own perceptions and beliefs about students.

Mental Models

Self-awareness helps foster stronger connections when teachers explore their beliefs, practices, and mental models about the students they serve. "*Mental models are the images, assumptions, and stories we carry in our minds of ourselves, other people, institutions, and every aspect of our world. Like a pane of glass framing and subtly distorting our vision, mental models determine what we see*" (Senge, 2006). Mental models capture how the mind represents real, remembered, hypothetical, or imaginary situations. They are rooted in belief instead of genuine concepts. Based on our experience, we believe that a connection exists between mental models, prejudices, implicit bias, and our actions. We should reflect on who we are, our experiences, and the opinions we have about others. It is critical to consider our beliefs as they impact and influence the manner in which we provide support to students. These are the defining statements we explore as we begin our equity journey.

The Mental Model and Implicit Bias Connection

Having educators look inwardly at their mental models builds knowledge around perceptions and biases and helps educators better understand themselves. We pose this question: How do the mental models, teacher expectations, and actions impact student achievement? Mental models can lead to prejudice and inflict implicit bias while stymying learning. For example, educators may not offer quality instructional activities to some students because they do not believe they can engage in meaningful experiments, debates, and problem-solving activities. In the previous example, the student, Mark, did not undertake a meaningful writing activity because he did not believe he could, nor initially did the teachers; however, when an adult believed in his abilities, he wrote a successful essay.

Furthermore, prejudging leads to preconceived opinions not based on reason or experience. Prejudging and holding those deficit beliefs can cause an educator to take negative actions, create biases, and even stifle students' learning opportunities. Biases are prejudices in favor of or against one thing, person, or group compared with another, usually in a way considered to be unfair. As educators, we can reflect on how we view colleagues, curriculum, instruction, and students to determine if we harbor biases. As we explore work around our mental models, a few questions can be implemented as a starting point for examining beliefs. See the Stop and Reflect section below. We use these questions during professional development workshops, teacher workshops, and staff meetings.

Stop and Reflect

Engage in deeper reflection on one or more of the questions below:

1. If you were to walk down the memory lane of your past life experiences, what childhood memories would you say informed your perspective about the students you serve?

2. What early messages were developed about school, literacy, and the capabilities of others?

3. What beliefs did you develop based on your upbringing?

4. Do any of those messages still influence you today?

5. How did you come to change your beliefs around previous messages received?

6. Did any of those messages enhance or hurt your life?

7. How do I demonstrate my belief in my students' intellectual abilities?

8. Can my students describe how I demonstrate my assumptions about their academic skills?

9. How do the learning activities, resources, and classroom environment reflect my beliefs about my students?

10. What tangible evidence am I using to support my views about my students?

11. How can I change what I am doing to acknowledge and recognize the academic potential of my students?

12. Do I see my students for who they are or who I want them to be?

Teachers' perceived biases and low expectations deny students the tools for academic success. We suggest starting with simple questions:

1. How am I building solid and lasting relationships with the students I serve?
2. Have I considered their trauma and the impact their experiences have on learning?
3. Do I believe that my students have the capacity for academic excellence?

Answering these questions offers a starting place for educators to address equity and build relationships in the classroom.

We contend that educators who combat antiracist practices and promote equity can improve learning, engagement, and a sense of belonging for students through equitable instruction. Utilizing the *SoLD* principles of *Systems of Support*, we extend learning opportunities for all students by removing barriers and creating healthy learning environments so the child's cognitive, social-emotional, and academic abilities can flourish.

Self-awareness helps foster stronger connections when teachers and instructional leaders explore their beliefs and practices in their interactions with students. Instructional leaders can also reflect and create conditions for educational equity across the school. Chart 2.1 provides a guide to equity that teachers and instructional leaders can implement.

Chart 2.1 • The Guide to Equity Literacy

Teacher Level
_____Engage in a Strengths, Weaknesses, Threats, and Opportunities (SWOT) analysis to determine the current state of your classroom in relation to meeting the academic and socioemotional needs of all your students
_____Self-explore mental models, lived experiences, and implicit bias
_____Assess classroom conditions for evidence of Equity, Diversity, and Belonging (Panorama Survey)
_____Get to know your student's interests and motivations (1:1 meetings)
_____Engage in book studies or read independently to build your cultural awareness using the suggested reading list
_____Build trusting student relationships (use Social Emotional Awareness, Trauma awareness, and Mindfulness strategies outlined in Appendices

_____Take action by writing an Equity Declaration or Equity Position Statement based on your *why*; provide quality instruction informed by the immediate learning needs of the students you serve

_____Monitor and reflect on the change you see in your classroom

_____Ensure rich experiences for all students (think about socioemotional and academic opportunities that build students' learning potential for whole-child education)

Instructional Leader/Coach Level

_____Engage in a Strengths, Weaknesses, Threats, and Opportunities (SWOT) analysis to determine the current state of your school or district concerning meeting the needs of all students

_____Determine the change agents necessary to carry out the work of educational equity and whole-child education

_____Determine "who" and "what" should be accomplished at your school or district (J. Collins, 2003)

_____Align staff on shared equity agreements (use Glenn Singleton's Four Courageous Agreements)

_____Engage staff in self-exploration and cultural awareness strategies as aligned to uncovering mental models, lived experiences, and implicit bias

_____Identify and create collective agreements around students' academic, and socioemotional needs

_____Ask each team member to share their *why* for equity and excellence for every child

_____Engage staff in self-reflection activities to uncover biases about the students they serve

_____Align on collective commitments that ensure every child feels seen and heard

_____Draft an Equity and Inclusion Declaration statement that embraces the voices of everyone in the school

_____Ensure alignment of the Equity and Inclusion Declaration to the Mission and Vision of the school and district

_____Review as a school the disciplinary and academic decisions to ensure alignment to the shared Equity and Inclusion Declaration

_____Use the shared Equity and Inclusion Declaration statement as road map that drives all academic, climate, and culture decisions

Recommended Reading for Building Equity Literacy

1. *The Right to Learn* (Darling-Hammond, 1997)
2. *Visible Learning* (Hattie, 2008)
3. *Visible Learning: The Sequel* (Hattie, 2023)
4. *Other People's Children* (Delpit, 1995)

(Continued)

(Continued)

Recommended Reading for Building Equity Literacy
5. *For White Folks Who Teach in the Hood* (Emdin, 2016)
6. *We Want to Do More Than Just Survive: Abolitionist Teaching and the Pursuit of Educational Freedom* (Love, 2019)
7. *Avoiding Equity Detours* (Gorski, 2019)
8. *Street Data* (Safir & Dugan, 2021)
9. *Dreamkeepers* (Ladson-Billings, 2009)
10. *Courageous Conversations* (Singleton, 2014)
11. *Cultivating Genius* (Muhammad, 2021)
12. *Belonging Through a Culture of Dignity* (Floyd & Kronapple, 2019)
13. *How to Be Antiracist* (Kendi, 2019)
14. *Culturally Responsive Teaching and the Brain* (Hammond, 2014)
15. *Understanding Your Instructional Power: Curriculum and Language Decisions to Support Each Student* (Reed-Marshall, 2023)

Source: © Equity Matters (2022).

So let's begin by evaluating our own lived experiences to assess the perceptions and biases we could hold about the students we serve. Stigmatized students may adjust their expectations and behavior to conform to teachers' negative biases (Ferguson, 2003). As a result, stigmatized students perform poorly because their teachers expect them to. Skillful teaching is the significant effect size variable for students to succeed in school. Educators must have the right mindset, materials, attitudes, and access to resources to accelerate students' learning experiences. Figure 2.4 provides a practical road map to engaging in self-awareness for educational equity.

Figure 2.4 • *(My Self-Awareness) a Self-Exploration Journey to Equity Literacy*

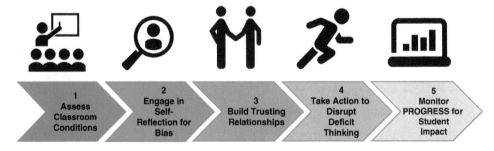

Source: © Sonya Murray (2022). Images courtesy of iStock.com/browndogstudios.

Setting a solid foundation for every child demands educators start with assessing their classroom conditions and self-reflecting to ensure we see students for who they are and not who we think they should be. Initially, the teachers in Story From the Field #2 did not recognize Mark Doe's talents, skills, or abilities; as a result, he could not rise above their perceptions and biases. Teachers taking the time to build a relationship with him unlocked the key to his potential. If we desire to serve students well, we should start on a meaningful journey that recognizes the biases that may transpire in our climates, cultures, and minds about students and their families.

Stop and Reflect

1. How has your view of the world influenced your teaching?
2. How are you building trusting relationships with your students?

THE IMPORTANCE OF TEACHER–STUDENT RELATIONSHIPS TO ACCELERATED LEARNING

"Teachers who foster positive relationships with their students create classroom environments more conducive to learning and to meeting students' developmental, emotional, and academic needs" (Rimm-Kaufman & Sandilos, 2015). A major component of the *SoLD* Principles for learning acceleration is creating a supportive environment in which children experience trust and connection within the classroom and between the school and their families. We contend that to advance learning, educators must create an environment where students are active participants in the learning community. Building relationships alone is not enough; authors Floyd Cobb and John Kronapple (2020) contend educators should also create opportunities for belonging. *"Belonging is the soil that nurtures inclusion and engagement. Educators want to create brave spaces to wrestle with issues through authentic spaces where students can risk being uncomfortable. A culture of belonging means that students are:*

1. *Appreciated and included*
2. *Validated and recognized; given voice*
3. *Accepted as they are without compromising identity*
4. *Treated fairly and given safety"* (Cobb & Krownapple, 2020)

Trauma, Learning, and Relationships

LeeAnn Gray (2016) reminds us that *educational trauma is the inadvertent perpetration of schools' harmful systemic and cyclical practices.* The focus for learning should be on the academic, cognitive, physical, psychological, and social-emotional development of the whole child (Darling-Hammond, 2020). We support the interconnectedness of the SoLD principles (Figure 2.5) as an effective approach for meeting the needs of the whole child. Educators can use the SoLD principles as they begin the equity journey of building solid relationships with students.

In our Story From the Field #2, Mark was experiencing trauma in his school and personal life. Joel Ristuccia (2018) of the Trauma and Learning Policy Initiative declares that trauma can directly impact a student's ability to learn and undermine their ability to form and maintain positive relationships with adults and their peers. Students who experience trauma exhibit the following behaviors: (a) lack of trust, (b) difficulty in interpreting verbal/nonverbal information, (c) poor sense of self and perspective-taking, (d) decreased motivation to relate to others, and (e) lack insight into relationships (Ristuccia, 2018). We have witnessed many students like Mark who are experiencing trauma and, as a result, face numerous challenges in learning and forming relationships. Educators who want to build positive relationships with students, reduce the effects of trauma, and promote learning need to embrace the tenets of trauma-sensitive schools. Trauma-sensitive schools, whose mission centers on trauma's impact on learning, build a climate and culture where all students feel safe, supported, and welcomed (Cole et al., 2013; Jones et al., 2018). We offer practical strategies and tips in our Take Action section at the end of the chapter to support educators using the SoLD principles to build solid relationships, recognizing students' need for social and emotional awareness. We assert that teachers who develop trusting relationships with students can positively or adversely affect their expectations of students and their capabilities.

> **Relationships power electricity to the brain, and the relationship between students and teachers are critical.**
> **—Pamela Cantor (2021)**

We agree with Dr. Cantor that relationships spark students' thinking, which makes learning more relevant and enjoyable. Students learn from people they enjoy being around. Dr. James P. Comer (1996), a leading educational psychiatrist, contends that *"no significant learning can happen in schools without positive relationships."* We agree and speak extensively about the importance of educator and student relationships, raising the importance of educators understanding their students through a lens of equity, compassion, and socio-emotional wellness.

We support teachers by embracing the *SoLD* principles and recognizing the need for whole-child development in the educational program (Figure 2.5). The *SoLD* principles are addressed because they indicate how environmental

Figure 2.5 • *SoLD Principles of Practices*

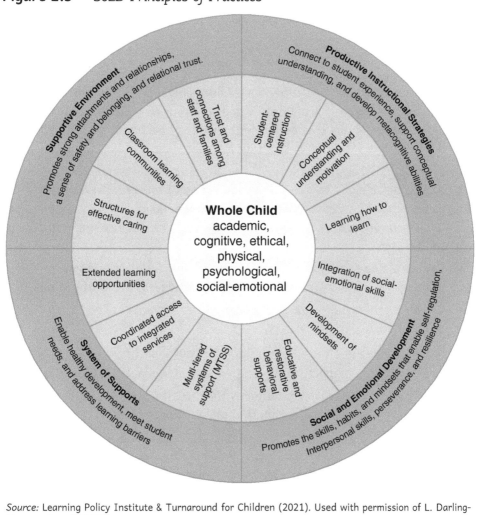

Source: Learning Policy Institute & Turnaround for Children (2021). Used with permission of L. Darling-Hammond et al. (2021).

factors, learning opportunities, and relationships shape learning. Five key elements are used: (a) positive developmental relationships, (b) environments filled with safety and belonging, (c) rich learning experiences and knowledge development, (d) development of positive skills, habits, and mindsets, and (e) integrated support systems (Learning Policy Institute & Turnaround for Children, 2021). The *SoLD* principles include evidence-based strategies that help students connect to their experiences, promote conceptual understanding, and improve their metacognitive abilities. Darling-Hammond maintains that the *SoLD* principles implement real change and promote equity; educators must provide a supportive environment, offer effective instruction, utilize a support system, and embrace social and emotional development (Darling-Hammond et al., 2020).

Specific structures aligned to SoLD principles that educators can take include but are not limited to

- Respecting students and coupling instruction that builds on students' cultures, identities, and experiences alongside efforts to reduce implicit and explicit bias in the classroom and school as a whole; these practices include affirmations that establish the value of each student, cultivate diversity as a resource, and encourage asset-based celebrations of accomplishments.
- Attending to signs of trauma using a range of tools and resources to understand what students are experiencing and healing-oriented practices, including mindfulness, counseling, and access to resources.
- Implementing shared values and norms framed as "do's" that guide relationships (e.g., respect, responsibility, kindness) rather than "don'ts."
- Creating opportunities for staff collaboration, structures, and consistent routines.
- Ensuring opportunities for shared decision-making.
- Communicating respect, caring and valuing of students and families.
- Implementing classroom strategies that counteract stereotype threat through cultural affirmation and reinforcement of students' capabilities.
- Fostering collaboration skills for building productive relationships among staff and with families and additional resources (Learning Policy Institute & Turnaround for Children, 2021).

Stop and Reflect

1. Which of the *SoLD* Principles are you actively incorporating into your classrooms? (a) Productive Instructional Strategies, (b) Social and Emotional Development, (c) Systems of Support, (d) Supportive Environment.

2. Which of the *SoLD* Principles are you currently downplaying, ignoring, or unable to integrate into the teaching and learning occurring in your classroom? (a) Productive Instructional Strategies, (b) Social and Emotional Development, (c) Systems of Support, (d) Supportive Environment.

RECOGNIZING AND RESPECTING STUDENTS' DIVERSE BACKGROUNDS

An educator desiring to make a lasting impact on students can start by forming relationships using a lens of equity and whole-child development. Educators can implement the concept of "Warm Demander" by Lisa Delpit (2012) and Zaretta Hammond (2015). Alexander (2016) contends that "Warm Demanders are teachers who, in the words of author Lisa Delpit, expect a great deal of their students, convince them of their brilliance, and help them to reach their potential in a disciplined and structured environment." Determining the climate in the class requires input from both the teacher and the students. We believe that students play a vital role in their own learning and can provide insight into the conditions under which they learn best. Assessing the climate for learning can be achieved by asking all students to complete or answer survey questions in which they indicate the following:

The things that I like best about our class are _____.

I feel good in class when _____.

I am encouraged to give my thoughts and opinions in class.

When I do not understand something, my teacher willingly helps me.

These are the three things that I like best about being in my class: _____.

These are the three things that I like least about being in my class: _____.

My classroom is a good place to learn. (Yes, No)

Assessing the classroom structures requires the teacher to look at their classroom from an outsider's perspective. In examining the systems, classroom teachers need to explore how they provide:

1. Academic support for all students.
2. Physical as well as emotional safety and well-being for all students.
3. Establishing classroom dynamics so that interpersonal relationships can quickly develop between students and teachers.
4. Engaging each of their students in building social, emotional, and civic skills, and finally, connecting the class to the more excellent physical surroundings of the school and the community.

Take Action

Now that you have explored mindset, perceptions, and steps to take to serve students' educational equity, act on your learning by completing the following applications.

Read, Respond, and Reflect

- Reread Story From the Field #2, and think about the comments:
- *"Have you met Mark yet? You are in for a rude awakening. He doesn't engage in school or complete any of his assignments.*
- *He is highly disruptive, and he angrily punched a hole through the wall of a detention room door two years ago."*

Let's Reflect

- How do you assess preconceived notions you may hold about the students you serve?
- What strategies do you currently utilize to build relationships with students?
- Do you see your student for their true potential independent of bias, and are your actions congruent?

Respond

- How can you best support students with challenging behaviors and academics?
- Do you listen to students and assess the circumstances before taking action?
- How are you connecting academics and socio-emotional development?
- In what ways could you build meaningful relationships with students?

> **Take Action**
>
> **How would you respond to the following statements?**
>
> Statement 1: "They need to pull up their pants...they just are not serious about school, and they won't get jobs like that."
>
> Statement 2: "Some students are just beyond helping!"
>
> Statement 3: "I institute zero tolerance in my classroom or school."
>
> Statement 4: "Our kids' parents don't believe in education, especially college education."
>
> Statement 5: "Parents should be teaching behaviors, not teachers."

SUMMARY

Equity in education is achievable through self-exploration of beliefs and practices, assessing students' learning environments, building trusting relationships, providing quality instruction, monitoring student progress, and creating positive socio-emotional experiences for learners and staff. Just as soup on a menu is nourishing, fulfilling, and enriching, relationships support our students' cognitive, emotional, and developmental needs. Equity occurs through action, reflection, and relationship building. Both teachers and students contribute to creating classroom climates for learning. Educators who promote equity embrace the *SoLD* principle of Social and Emotional Development. They provide learners with the skills needed to build habits, relationships, and mindsets that enable self-regulation, resilience, and perseverance as these learners encounter challenging learning activities. This chapter provides a menu educators can use to build solid student relationships. The first step is to acknowledge how all students in the class are viewed or perceived. Next, teachers engage in an exploration of their own lived experiences and mindsets. Finally, teachers may select resources for building equitable classroom practices, learning activities, and student engagement.

 TIME TO DIG IN TOOLS

Activity	Description	Research Support and Reference	Link
National Center on Intensive Intervention	The center provides information and resources on effective academic and behavioral intervention programs, including research reviews of intervention programs, to assist with selecting an evidence-based approach based on a school or district's needs.	https://intensiveintervention.org/	https://qrs.ly/nbeqdz5
Turnaround for Children	This organization produces research-based tools for practitioners, such as a toolkit on how to use a whole-child vision to assess and plan for tiered systems of support and resources to inform a school critical plan to accelerate healthy student development and academic achievement. The toolkit can help educators use a whole-child vision to assess and plan for Tier 2 and Tier 3 systems.	https://turnaroundusa.org/	https://qrs.ly/v8eqdzc

Activity	Description	Research Support and Reference	Link
Collaborative for Academic, Social, and Emotional Learning Integrate Student Supports with School-wide SEL	CASEL offers a comprehensive collection of high-quality social and emotional learning tools and resources to inform and support educators, researchers, and policymakers. And parents who are learning this work in the field.	www.casel.org	https://www.casel.org
Panorama Education	Panorama Education partners with K–12 schools and districts across the country to collect and analyze data about social emotional learning, school climate, family engagement, and more.	A multitude of resources to address student's socioemotional awareness, needs (mindfulness strategies, trauma, and an equity lens)	https://qrs.ly/lxeqdzk
The Comer Project	The Comer Child Development Program	https://qrs.ly/bceqdzz	https://qrs.ly/y4eqe0a
Learning for Justice (formerly Teaching Tolerance)	Trauma Responsive-Education-Supporting-Students-and-Yourself	Thomas, M. S., Crosby, S., & Vanderhaar, J. (2019). Trauma-informed practices in Schools across two decades: An interdisciplinary review of research. *Review of Research in Education, 43*(1), 422–452. https://doi.org/10.3102/0091732X18821123	https://qrs.ly/pjeqdtq

(Continued)

(Continued)

Activity	Description	Research Support and Reference	Link
Rose, Thorn, Bud Reflection Activity	The rose, thorn, bud reflection activity offers rich ways for teachers, leaders, and students to reflect using mindfulness.	Mindful Schools Argos Gonzalez	https://qrs.ly/jdeqe0n
CABI Cultural Attitudes and Belief Inventory	Inventory measures the perceptions and attitudes of urban teachers' cultural awareness and beliefs.	Natesan, P., Webb-Hasan, G., Carter, N., & Walter, P. (2014). Validity of the cultural awareness and beliefs inventory of urban teachers: A parallel mixed methods study. *International Journal of Multiple Research Approaches, 5,* 238–253. https://doi.org/10.5172/mra.2011.5.2.238	https://qrs.ly/6eeqe0t
Panorama 21 Questions to Connect with Students	Panorama provides a wealth of free research-based surveys to educators on a variety of topics.	www.panoramaed.com	https://qrs.ly/hreqdu0
Equity Literacy for All	Paul Gorski and Kathy Swalwell (2015) provide a series of resources for extending equity literacy. http://edchange.org/publications/Equity-Literacy-for-All.pdf	Gorski, P. (April 2019). Avoiding equity detours. *Education Leadership, 76*(7), 56–71.	https://qrs.ly/jqeqe1n

Activity	Description	Research Support and Reference	Link
Transforming Mindfulness Toolkit	Transforming Education	Zenner, C., Herrnleben-Kurz, S., & Walach, H. (2014). Mindfulness-based interventions in schools—A systematic review and meta-analysis. *Frontiers in Psychology*, 603. https://www.frontiersin.org/articles/10.3389/fpsyg.2014.00603/full	https://qrs.ly/gyeqe1p

CHAPTER 3

THE APPETIZER

Surveying Curriculum and Data Sources

> I suggest that the problem is rooted in how we think about the social contexts, the students, the curriculum, and instruction.
> —Gloria Ladson Billings

Figure 3.1 • *Murray and Turner's (2021) Five-Course Framework for Accelerated Learning*

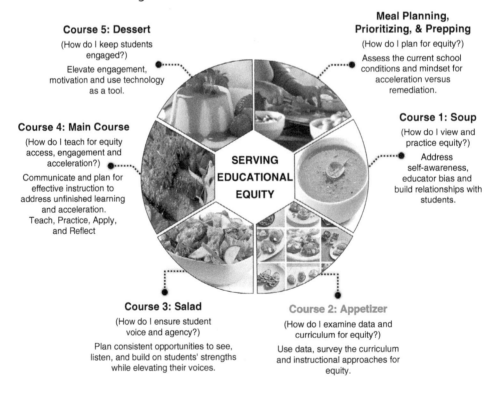

Course 5: Dessert
(How do I keep students engaged?)
Elevate engagement, motivation and use technology as a tool.

Meal Planning, Prioritizing, & Prepping
(How do I plan for equity?)
Assess the current school conditions and mindset for acceleration versus remediation.

Course 4: Main Course
(How do I teach for equity access, engagement and acceleration?)
Communicate and plan for effective instruction to address unfinished learning and acceleration.
Teach, Practice, Apply, and Reflect

Course 1: Soup
(How do I view and practice equity?)
Address self-awareness, educator bias and build relationships with students.

SERVING EDUCATIONAL EQUITY

Course 3: Salad
(How do I ensure student voice and agency?)
Plan consistent opportunities to see, listen, and build on students' strengths while elevating their voices.

Course 2: Appetizer
(How do I examine data and curriculum for equity?)
Use data, survey the curriculum and instructional approaches for equity.

CHAPTER THREE

- Highlights the importance of educators surveying their curriculum for alignment to standards, rigor, and coherence, analogous to a meal taker selecting appetizers for consumption based on their palate.
- Discusses the connection between curriculum, data, assessment, and feedback for learning acceleration.
- Outlines the importance of scaffolding grade level, high-quality curricula to support students' accelerated learning.

Appetizers present an opportunity to sample tasty morsels before a hearty meal. Our multi-course meal analogy allows for the examination of both data and curriculum to determine equity as a part of the appetizer course; see Figure 3.1. The chef selects and prepares appetizers that complement the meal choices. Educators should engage in a similar process when selecting the curriculum they will use for their students. Surveying the curriculum is essential to instructional recovery while advancing student learning. The Curriculum *is a general term that includes all the learning materials and strategies used to support student achievement of the standards* (Florida Education Foundation, 1984). This chapter allows us to embrace the *SoLD* principle of designing *Productive Instructional Strategies* in which we focus on learning experiences, resources, and materials that connect to the student's experiences while supporting conceptual understanding as these students develop metacognitive abilities. This chapter addresses the *SoLD* principle of appropriate *Systems of Support*, in which multi-tiered systems of support and learning barriers are addressed. The curriculum, resources, and activities are designed to accelerate students' learning.

Review Story From the Field #4 and consider how these educators might consider using their curriculum for learning acceleration.

Story From the Field #4

As I sat in a principal's office waiting for a coaching meeting in a diverse, urban school district, I overheard teachers holding very familiar conversations about their student's abilities while surveying their newly adopted curriculum, the students, and the school's academic data. One teacher says, *"Our data doesn't show that students mastered the skills from our most recent assessment, and the curriculum is not designed to meet them where they are."* *"Our*

students will hate this new curriculum. I think it is too hard for my students."
Another teacher continues, *"This curriculum is not easy to teach and will be virtually impossible to implement for our students. Many of my kids are already performing below grade level."* While another teacher states, "We *are constantly required to learn a new curriculum when it takes dedicated time to implement one."* The conversations concluded with teachers proposing to return to their original curriculum, even though the students were not assessed for mastery of taught skills. The teachers predicted students would not be capable of learning the new, challenging curriculum, and their deficit thinking became a self-fulfilling prophecy.

These statements in Story From the Field #4 are not unique to this group of educators. Others across the country echo the sentiments expressed by these teachers. We recall countless experiences in which educators are charged with providing students access to complex, grade-level materials when students are not ready. We hear these remarks and assert they are focused on three key issues crucial to educational change (Figure 3.2):

1. Teachers' beliefs in their students' learning deficits and limitations.
2. Teacher's lack of confidence in teaching the curriculum.
3. Teachers' challenges in providing instruction that reaches mastery for all students.

Figure 3.2 • *Where to Begin? Equity and the Curriculum*

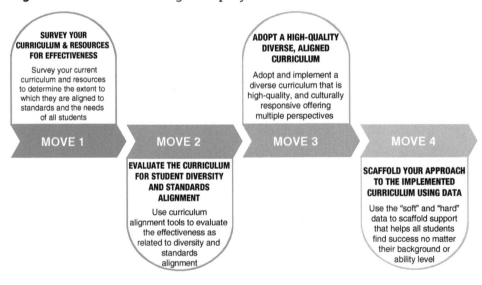

Stop and Reflect

How does Story From the Field #4 resonate with your thinking about your current curriculum and how you use it to accelerate students' learning?

Ask yourself:

1. Are my beliefs and assumptions about the curriculum supported by data? Do my beliefs in my students' abilities affect my curriculum choices?

2. Does my feedback to students accelerate their learning?

3. Do I have a deficit thinking about students, their performance, and the materials I choose in making pedagogical decisions?

4. Do I provide instruction that aligns with our curriculum?

Story From the Field #5

In visiting another one of our schools for a coaching meeting, it was shared that the district was exploring a new mathematics curriculum. The current curriculum was seven years old and would need to be replaced. Teachers were asked to give their input on the best curriculum to adopt based on their students' academic needs. Teachers grappled with this task, deciding that the best way to determine the most effective curriculum for their students would be to look at the students' hard and soft data. "Hard data," such as numerical data and test scores, should be supported by "soft data" that explores beliefs, perceptions, and practices.

Stop and Reflect

1. Have you ever been asked to implement a new curriculum? How was that experience?

2. What was your approach? How did you feel? What actions did you take to initiate the process?

THE CURRICULUM EVALUATION AND ALIGNMENT

Students need access to a high-quality curriculum as a pivotal approach to student learning acceleration, as an appetizer is to the meal course. We believe curricular materials are the ideal vehicle for advancing student learning. High-quality, grade-level curricula align with students' critical skills for college and career success. We agree with Barbara Blackburn that expecting every student to learn at high levels begins with the curriculum or content of your lesson (Blackburn, 2008). Teachers would benefit from selecting and implementing a curriculum with fidelity researched by experts, as informed by student data. This critical phase of the five-course meal—the appetizer—allows the diners to survey and select what they would like based on their palate. The analogy to serving educational equity here is that educators should choose from high-quality materials for guidance, acceleration, and reimagining teaching and learning.

We believe that it is the schools' responsibility to select high-quality materials. We assert that educators should take this pivotal step following deep reflection on their own potential biases and perceptions about the students they serve. In addition, teachers should utilize the curriculum as a resource that helps them get students to master academic content. We connect to the educator's mindset around implementing a high-quality curriculum and using data to keep a grade-level focus. We hear critical questions from educators: "*How do I utilize a high-quality curriculum and grade-level content with students performing below grade level?*" "*How can I ensure students master grade-level skills when they are low-performing?*" "*What is the best curriculum to use when I want to help students find success? We want to offer strategies for scaffolding the curriculum and focusing on student needs, but there is prevalent learning loss.*" We must provide students access to grade-level materials to prepare for college and careers, regardless of their ability level. Since the impact of an aligned curriculum equates to eight months of additional learning for middle school students (Kane et al., 2016), we assert that the time to address this need is now.

Curriculum alignment is an academic term that incorporates local academic *standards, educational programs, instructional materials, teaching techniques, and academic assessments that are all coordinated within schools* (Elsworth, 2020). It is how teachers organize and present content in the classroom, including what they teach, how they teach it, and how they assess learning. It is how written content, instruction, and assessment work together to facilitate student achievement as defined by standards. We support the conclusion that aligning the curriculum to the standards improves teaching and learning. The school succeeds when a team of educators set commonly aligned goals and determines what they want their students to accomplish. Whether students are mastering a specific skill or grasping a set of standards, success happens when everyone is on the same page and knows what they want to accomplish (Muir, 2018). We make the connection to the curriculum as an appetizer, as educators have an opportunity to choose the curriculum or parts of the curriculum that can help them recover student learning as informed by data.

Equity and the Curriculum

An equity approach to curriculum design benefits all students (Samuel, 2019). When the curriculum is aligned, it assures that all students have an equitable education based on high standards. Also, it provides a clear presentation of the standards at each grade level and subject area. Finally, curriculum alignment assures that instruction at each grade level and subject area is on target.

When we think of a design for an equitable curriculum, we envision curricula that are analogous to Dr. Rudine Sims Bishop's (1990) *Mirrors, Windows, and Sliding Glass Door* examples. Curricula materials, topics, and tasks should engage students in exploring their own lives and experiences as well as the identities and cultures of others. Students should engage in curricula materials, topics, and tasks that "*mirror*" and reflect their own lives, interests, and experiences. When the curriculum presents materials, topics, and tasks that allow students to see others or look through "*windows*" to see new worlds, they can engage in empathy respect and determine how they are connected to others. Finally, when the curriculum provides access or "*sliding glass doors*" for students to walk through, they are exposed to a greater world.

We support Samuel's (2019) assertions that equity in curricula provides three critical benefits for students:

1. *Enriches language, reasoning, writing, discussion, and literacy skills by creating opportunities for conversations on different perspectives and challenging belief systems.*
2. *Increases engagement among students by helping them feel connected to a curriculum that honors their story and background.*
3. *Improves school climate and safety by giving students a sense of belonging and collective responsibility in the classroom (p. 2).*

In their *Equity and Inclusion Framework for Curriculum Design*, Alozie et al. (2021) present an evidence-centered design to STEM curricula that focuses on the diverse needs of students and suggests that educators explore how students are responding to the curriculum through a series of questions that are presented in the following Stop and Reflect segment.

Stop and Reflect

How are students responding to the curriculum?

1. Are they engaged?
2. Are they excited to learn?
3. Do students apply what they learn to real-world situations?
4. Do students feel safe and valued in the class as they learn through the curriculum?
5. Are students actively participating in conversations related to concepts?
6. Are students fostering critical thinking and knowledge transferring?
7. Are students becoming interested in learning more about the concepts?

Source: Equity and Inclusion Framework for Curriculum Design (Alozie et al., 2021).

We believe that exploring these questions will not only help in improving the curricular offerings but also provide opportunities to welcome students' voices, comments, and perspectives on what they are learning.

The Organization for Economic Co-Operation and Development (OECD) (2021) has researched curricular designs that embrace equity. OECD (2021) identifies four curricular designs that embrace equity: Digital, Personalized, Cross-curricular Content and Competency-based, and Flexible. Many schools are utilizing aspects of each. Digital curricular design embraces technology such as screen readers and voice recognition applications to assist students who are engaged in remote learning and those with special needs. A personalized curriculum focuses on individualized learning goals and plans, which are matched with relevant content choices and activities. The focus is on tailoring materials and instruction that match the students' needs, skills, and interests. Cross-curricular content and competency-based emphasize the importance of interdisciplinary knowledge and engage in practical learning in which students connect their knowledge across different disciplines. A major emphasis is on integrated learning and inquiry-based learning. A flexible curriculum allows schools and educators to make local decisions about their curriculum, including the content, goals, assessments, and instruction as the time and place of learning (OECD, 2021).

In Story From the Field #4, one teacher lamented about the deficiencies in the curriculum but appeared to be powerless to address those deficiencies. Curriculum alignment is critical because it shows how the all components of an education system (standards, assessments, resources, instruction, and learning activities) work together to achieve the school's desired goals. When the curriculum is aligned, it can provide a seamless pathway/transition for students to advance through their education program and improve student achievement (Squires, 2012). *A high-quality curriculum includes lessons that empower students and develop their critical thinking and communication skills, creating a classroom culture that nurtures students' leadership and agency and encourages critical analysis of the world. Such a curriculum allows us to put equity into action day in and day out* (Hartl & Riley, 2021). Since students from low-income communities are less likely to access high-quality content and textbooks, the curriculum focus could be a tactical step to advance educational equity (VanTassel-Baska, 2017). As an ongoing examination of their current curricula, we recommend that teachers evaluate the critical features of their curriculum to ensure that it is aligned. Pete Rogan (2017) suggests these alignment features:

1. *Connection to standards*
2. *Relevance activities*
3. *Flexibility*
4. *Variety in the instructional approaches*
5. *Active student engagement*
6. *Rigor needed for academic advancement*

Surveying the Curriculum

In Story From the Field #5, teachers were tasked with providing their input on selecting the district's new curriculum. It would be pivotal that educators understand the importance of this decision. Thomas Kane of the Harvard Center for Education Policy Research (Kane et al., 2016) reports that the impact of a moderately aligned curriculum is almost as much as replacing a teacher in the 50th percentile with a teacher in the 75th percentile. The difference between a moderately aligned and a misaligned curriculum equates to about eight months of additional learning for a middle school student.

Stop and Reflect

1. Why might it be essential to implement a rigorous curriculum?

2. In what ways could a rigorous curriculum enhance student learning?

As teachers engage in proactive approaches that ensure rigor in their curriculum, they can utilize supports such as *EdReports*, their expertise, and student data to determine the quality of their curriculum. EdReports is an independent nonprofit committed to providing all students access to high-quality instructional materials. EdReports publishes free reviews of K–12 instructional materials using an educator-led approach that measures standards alignment, usability, research-based practices, and other quality criteria. Using EdReports can help educators better understand when curriculum lacks rigor and is weak in helping achieve content goals. The teachers in Stories From the Field #4 and #5 would benefit from analyzing their curricula with the tools.

Stop and Reflect

1. Think about your curriculum. Is it rigorous? Does it help you meet the needs of your students? Take a moment to place your curriculum in the **EdReports.org** tool to assess rigor, relevance, and coherence. What did you find out about your current curriculum?

2. Using your reflection, does your curriculum serve your student population?

Evaluating Curriculum for Learning Advancement

Educators will also want to evaluate curriculum alignment for relevance and learning advancement. We suggest using Peter Rogan's Evaluation Criteria as a guide. Rogan (2017) provides six key areas for evaluating curriculum: (a) *Alignment*, (b) *Relevance*, (c) *Flexibility*, (d) *Instruction*, (e) *Engagement*, and (f) *Rigor*. Educators should ensure that the curriculum is aligned with their state and professional standards and that objectives can be met. The curriculum resources must provide sufficient coverage of key objectives and learning goals. Educators should explore the relevance of materials and lessons in meeting the needs of both learners and teachers. Posing questions such as *"Why are certain topics addressed?"* and *"Why are we learning these concepts?"* helps to connect the topics to the lives of the learners. Instruction using the curriculum materials, lessons, and resources need to support a range of delivery modes, including face-to-face, distance, small group interactive, full class, individual, direct, and indirect. Instruction needs to focus on the needs of the learners to advance their learning. Curriculum materials, resources, and lessons need to support the active engagement of the learners as well as learner autonomy and ongoing support. Finally, curriculum materials, resources, and lessons must possess the rigor that allows each student a depth of understanding as reflected in the standards. The materials must include accurate content and quality assessments and engage students in meaningful learning (Rogan, 2017).

Stop and Reflect

1. Are you currently using an aligned curriculum in your school or classroom?

2. How are you using soft and hard data to make decisions about the best curriculum to use?

DATA AND THE CURRICULUM

Starting with an honest examination of the data can help educators make informed decisions about their curriculum. We do not believe that only "hard data" such as test scores should be examined; we support an honest appraisal of "soft data" that explores beliefs, perceptions, and practices. Too often, we might think assessment scores and attendance reports are the only legitimate data for decision-making. Examining the assessment scores, formal assessments, informal assessments, and attendance reports are common practices in data analysis. However, instead of focusing on weaknesses, it is imperative to look at strengths and authentic, real-time information. In addition to examining standardized measures, an educator can do quick informal readings, quick checks of content knowledge and skill applications, and formative assessments. If students struggle to master the grade-level content, teachers can begin by exploring students' misconceptions, strengths, and weaknesses as they plan their instruction. Starting with crucial, real-time data allows teachers to effectively plan and deliver just-in-time instruction. In the next section, we discuss how data can be utilized as a driving force in curricular decision-making. Closely examining our beliefs, perceptions, and practices can provide valuable data essential to determining the best resources, assessment strategies, and curricula to accelerate student learning.

Stop and Reflect

1. Are you using hard and soft data to examine your beliefs, perceptions, practices, and actions connected to curriculum choices?

2. How could you use the *Skill, Will, or Thrill* resource to determine where your students fall based on anecdotal hard and soft data?

Identify students in your classroom and sort them into three categories reflecting on hard and soft data. These categories can assist in acknowledging the strengths that students bring to the learning tasks. They are based on the Model of Learning (Hattie & Donoghue, 2016), and they have been used in advancing reading comprehension (Fisher & Frey, 2020). Reflect on ways you can provide students with accelerated learning opportunities, reflecting on their progress or lack of skills as **SKILL, WILL, or THRILL**.

Concepts can be introduced without giving students the opportunities to master, practice, and apply those concepts. Figure 3.3 emphasizes the difference between teaching or introducing concepts and actual learning. The two small children and a dog reflect on teaching a dog named Buddy to read. In the first frame, the girl says, "I taught Buddy to read." The boy responds, "I don't hear him reading," in the second frame. In the final frame, the girl says, "I taught him. I didn't say he learned it." We love this cartoon as it perfectly represents what can happen in classrooms and schools across the country when teaching occurs without being accompanied by learning. Teaching with mastery can be implemented, and we encourage you to consider "intent" versus "impact." We encourage educators to shift their mindset to reflect more on how students learn and less on covering skills.

Skill	Will	Thrill
Students who try to engage academically and socially but struggle with specific skill areas making academic progress challenging.	Students who are disengaged in the learning process but have the talent and ability to perform at high levels academically.	Students who are thriving academically and socially. These students are holistically engaged in the learning process.
Students	Students	Students
Evidence	Evidence	Evidence
How can you engage students in the learning process? What types of acceleration practices can be implemented?	What acceleration and engagement strategies could be utilized to increase their learning?	How can you accelerate their learning and sustain engagement to maximize their learning?

Source: © Murray (2021).

Figure 3.3 • *Introducing Concepts or Teaching for Mastery*

Source: Adapted from Blake (1967). Image courtesy of iStock.com/Lisitsa.

We embrace a Mastery Teaching and a Learning Cycle, which focuses on a system of planning, teaching, assessing, analyzing, revisiting, and reflecting. Educators who use the curriculum's learning targets and standards focus their instruction, learning activities, and resources so that students are provided equitable instruction at high levels. The Cycle presents a strong focus on planning, teaching, assessing, surveying, modifying instruction, reflecting, re-evaluating, and reteaching skills for students to succeed. This model recognizes the importance of allowing students to master skills through reflection and scaffolding. The emphasis is on providing acceleration for learning (Figure 3.4).

Figure 3.4 • *Mastery Teaching and Learning Visual*

1. Plan from learning targets

 Start planning from learning targets and standards.

4. Analyze the data

 Analyze the data and student work for misconceptions and areas of strength.

2. Teach high levels

 Instruct all students at high levels, no matter their skills or ability level.

5. Revisit instructional approaches

 Use the student misconceptions to revisit and adapt previously used instructional strategies.

3. Assess

Use bias-free assessments that help students reach their full academic potential.

6. Reflect, modify, instruct, and reassess

 Reflect on the instructional approaches used, modify instruction, and reassess students.

Source: Images courtesy of iStock.com/browndogstudios.

 Stop and Reflect

1. Are there times you focus on covering the content instead of students' mastery of concepts?

2. What types of data are you using to drive instructional decisions?

With a focus on learning loss and addressing gaps in learning weighing heavily on the minds of educators, ways to address the needs of students will require a mindset shift. Shifting to what students need to access grade-level skills and how students learn can help educators embrace student learning in ways that help them find success. Consistency and practical routines such as the cadence can help educators combat the learning of isolated skills versus teaching for mastery issues, as outlined in Figure 3.5, highlights the importance of using data to drive instructional and curricular decisions. It also helps us reflect on ways we provide feedback and support to students. As we survey the data at this level, it becomes critical that we successfully address the balancing act of listening to soft and hard student data to drive decisions.

The cadence offers a systematic approach teachers and staff can utilize to allow data to drive their teaching and learning focus. For example, as

Figure 3.5 • *Cadence of Weekly Data Review*

Step 1	**Step 2**
Review the data from a recent assessment (engage in item analysis)	Analyze student work and analyze misconceptions to determine intervention and support
Step 3	**Step 4**
Teacher modeling and sharing of best practices with students on identified misconceptions	Teacher reflects and revisits instructional practices and student learning outcomes

teachers in Story From the Field #5 worked on reclaiming their students' loss of learning, they reviewed the data from one of their recent assessments and analyzed samples of their students' work to determine where misconceptions existed. The key feature was modeling to help students overcome or correct misconceptions. These teachers focused on these three questions: *What do we want students to learn? How will we know when each student has learned it? How can we improve on current levels of student achievement?* (DuFour et al., 2010). Using this information as a guide, they selected best practices built on students' experiences and offered modeling and scaffolding that allowed students to engage in various learning activities. Students applied their knowledge, and these teachers could reflect on the success of both the instruction and practice.

Stop and Reflect

1. Do you currently have a routine for how you use data to drive decisions?

2. How effective is this routine or process in helping you make curricular and instructional decisions?

Connecting Assessment, Grades, and Feedback to the Curriculum

There must be a clear connection between the curriculum standards, assessment, grading, and reporting systems. We contend that a variety of assessments should be an integral part of the curriculum. Teachers use assessments to determine if standards are being met if students are mastering content, and if instruction targets learning outcomes and goals. We believe that the assessment and feedback given to all students must be sound and effective; see Figure 3.6. We support teachers who want to be *assessment literate*. Laura Greenstein (2020) maintains that these teachers use their knowledge and skills to gather accurate information about their students and use this information in practical ways to inform and improve learning. Additionally, we conclude that student feedback needs to be timely, actionable, and relevant. We agree with Hanna Hart (2021), who maintains that "*feedback is most effective when it is grounded in a growth mindset and intended to promote learning, and understanding must be a clear connection between the curriculum standards, grading, and reporting systems.*" Grades result from teachers calculating, describing, and reporting on student performance (Hough, 2019). As educators, we have not always been consistent or fair in our grading practices for all students. Grade reporting needs to be valid, reliable, and fair and focus on students' mastery of the content and standards (Munoz & Guskey, 2015). Joe Feldman (2019) reminds us that equitable grading includes accuracy, is bias-resistant and engages one in intrinsic motivation.

Figure 3.6 • *Balancing Assessment Data and Feedback*

Stop and Reflect

1. Do you provide a variety of assessments including, formative, summative, informal, and teacher developed, and student self-assessments to guide instruction?

2. Do you connect your grades and feedback to your curriculum standards?

3. Do your students know what to do with the feedback that you provide?

Story From the Field #6

In one of the schools we support, teachers were asked to select materials to address students' areas of focus. Teachers talked about students' needs. They wanted a rigorous curriculum to address this concern. The teachers lacked appropriate resources and, after a review of the data summarized that more was required to meet students' needs.

We believe that teachers can incorporate a rigorous curriculum in their classrooms. This has to be done intentionally, and therefore, we highly recommend that educators purchase high-quality curriculum as a "low-hanging fruit" option and take time to reflect on ways the curriculum offers diversity and effective assessment practices to benefit all of their students.

In addition to surveying useful approaches to data and assessments, educators will want to establish the best approaches for selecting a high-quality curriculum. *A high-quality curriculum includes lessons that empower students and develop their critical thinking and communication skills, creating a classroom culture that nurtures students' leadership and agency and encourages critical analysis of the world. Such a curriculum gives us a way to put equity into action day in and day out* (Hartl & Riley, 2021).

Scaffolding Grade Level, High-Quality Curricula to Support Students' Accelerated Learning

In our own efforts to assist educators who want to ensure learning acceleration, we encourage utilizing the following approach to instructional recovery with any curriculum:

1. Determine the rigor and coherence of the curriculum by visiting EdReports.org for comparison and analysis.
2. Identify the focus and foundational standards for the module or units you teach.
3. Create a calendar that removes activities not connected to the central lesson objective unit that students could not master.
4. Make a list of the foundational units and prioritize those as supplements to the grade-level curriculum.
5. Shorten the time for assessment. Most curricula will budget 3–4 days per unit assessment. Decrease the time to one to two days to save time.

6. Leverage small group instruction opportunities (Tier II) and intensive instructional times (Tier III) to provide students with access to the grade-level curriculum as they need additional scaffolding: This approach can ensure the whole group moves on in the curriculum while other students get additional support. Tutors or extra volunteers can be instrumental in this regard, if possible.

7. Tighten late-year units. Think about the additional and supporting work and ways to condense the focus.

8. See Time for Tools section to utilize Chicago Public Schools Flashback-Forward Protocol to address missed content and curriculum.

9. Review Achieve the Core's Coherence Map. See Time for Tools, which is an excellent resource to address learning standards.

Take Action

Now that you have explored the importance of utilizing a high-quality curriculum, act on your learning by completing the following application.

Read, Respond, and Reflect

Reread Story From the Field #4 and think about the comments:

- *"How do I utilize a high-quality curriculum and grade-level content with students performing below grade level?"*
- *"How can I ensure students master grade-level skills when they are low-performing?"*

Let's Reflect

- Have you evaluated your current curriculum using EdReports (www.edreports.org)?
- How are you using student data to determine the most effective curriculum that accelerates students' learning?

Respond

- How can you use the current curriculum to accelerate student learning?
- What are the approaches you use to determine student mastery?
- What data cycle do you use to determine student mastery? Is your data cadence similar to the one in Figure 3.5? Why or why not?

SUMMARY

Advancing the academic abilities of students requires direct action by educators. Surveying the curriculum is important to instructional recovery while advancing student learning and one of the significant actions is to ensure the curriculum is aligned. Just as the choosing and sampling of appealing appetizers can complement a meal, surveying the curriculum and reviewing data can prepare for quality instruction and learning acceleration. When the curriculum is aligned, it provides a clear understanding of standards, ensures that instruction is on target, and assures that all students have an equitable education based on high standards. We believe that students excel when instruction meets their needs, and they engage in learning how to learn. Becoming assessment literate will allow educators to understand the connection between and across fair assessments, assessment instruments, feedback, and grades offered to advance student learning. In addition, conducting self-assessments, exploring students' formal and informal data, ensuring an aligned curriculum, and engaging students in authentic learning activities lead to accelerating students' learning. An aligned curriculum, fair assessments, and proper use of hard and soft data do not just happen; we know that equitable practices must be intentional.

 **TIME TO DIG IN TOOLS**

Activity	Description	Research Support and Reference	Link
Visit the EdReports.org website to enter your current curriculum	EdReports.org is an independent nonprofit that publishes free reviews of K–12 instructional materials, using an educator-led approach that measures standards alignment, usability, research-based practices, and other quality criteria.	www. edreports. org	https://www. edreports. org
Flash Back — Forward Protocol	The Flash Back — Flash Forward Protocol can be utilized to help teachers align to critical standards and curriculum to teach for student mastery.	Chicago Network 6 https:// docs.google.com/ document/d/ 1NWrJjldlO6qyI Hwdnilq3EqO-0psP-e9r2PxZMo1 hZw/edit	https:// qrs.ly/ yweqe28
Achieve the Core Coherence Map	The Achieve the Core coherence map tool is designed to illuminate the coherent connections of the standards.	Math Coherence Map	https:// qrs.ly/ hqeqe2f

Activity	Description	Research Support and Reference	Link
Sample Data Cadence Protocol	This protocol can be utilized to create a rhythm and clear process for providing teaching and learning that leads to student mastery.	Data Cadence	https://bit.ly/3Emnhoz
Priority Content in ELA and Mathematics	This document provides guidance for the field about content priorities by leveraging the structure and emphasis of college and career ready mathematics and ELA/literacy standards.	Priority Content in ELA and Mathematics	https://bit.ly/2LIDEF3
Feedback Checklist	Checklist on how to integrate effective feedback in the classroom.	The Education Hub	https://qrs.ly/z3eqe2k
Grading for Equity: Quiz for Teachers: How equitable is your grading?	Formative assessment that teachers can use to explore how accurate, bias-free, and motivational their classroom grading procedures are.	Feldman, J. (2019). *Grading for equity: What it is, why it matters, and how it can transform schools and classrooms.* Corwin.	https://qrs.ly/dieqe2u
Grading and Reporting for Educational Equity	Guide to highlight practices that schools can use to ensure that their grading and reporting systems are equitable.	Great School Partnership	https://qrs.ly/8reqe2x
Grading for Equity Toolkit	Resources, checklists, online courses, teacher examples.	Feldman, J. (2019). *Grading for equity.* Corwin.	https://www.gradingforequity.org

(Continued)

(Continued)

Activity	Description	Research Support and Reference	Link
Reciprocal Teaching	Students become the teacher and lead a small group during the session using summarizing, clarifying, generating questions, and predicting.	Oczuks, L. (2003). *Reciprocal teaching at work: Strategies for improving reading comprehension.* International Reading Association.	https://qrs.ly/5veqku9
Assessing Learning in the Classroom (National Education Association)	This book describes common principles for effective assessment that educators can use to ensure assessments inform teaching and learning. Authors describe various assessment approaches and their strengths and limitations using vignettes of effective classroom assessments in action.	National Education Association	https://eric.ed.gov/?id=ED429989
Equity and Inclusion Framework for Curriculum Design	The framework provides guiding questions, a planning guide, and design principles to determine if existing curriculum lessons integrate equity and inclusion for STEM Materials. The framework is guided by evidence-	The National Comprehensive Center. Alozie, N., Haugabook Pennock, P., Madden, K., Zaidi, S., Harris, C. J., & Krajcik, J. S. (2018). Designing and Developing NGSS-Aligned	https://www.compcenternetwork.org/ https://achievethecore.org/peersandpedagogy/a-process-

Activity	Description	Research Support and Reference	Link
	centered design methods.	Formative Assessment Tasks to Promote Equity [Paper presentation]. Annual conference of National Association for Research in Science Teaching, Atlanta, GA, United States.	to-address-unfinished-learning-in-middle-school-math/

CHAPTER 4

THE SALAD

Ensuring Student Agency, Diversity, and Voice

> Diversity is having a seat at the table, inclusion is
> having a voice, and belonging is having a voice be heard.
> —Fosslien and Duffy (2019)

Figure 4.1 • *Murray and Turner's (2021) Five-Course Framework for Accelerated Learning*

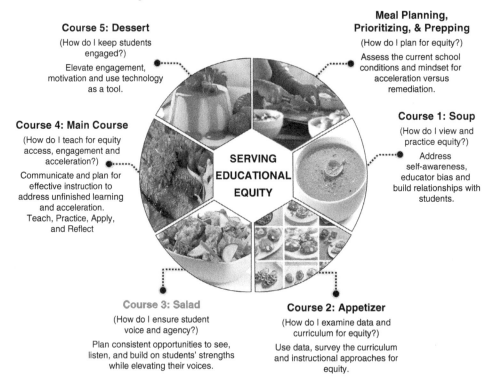

Course 5: Dessert
(How do I keep students engaged?)
Elevate engagement, motivation and use technology as a tool.

Meal Planning, Prioritizing, & Prepping
(How do I plan for equity?)
Assess the current school conditions and mindset for acceleration versus remediation.

Course 4: Main Course
(How do I teach for equity access, engagement and acceleration?)
Communicate and plan for effective instruction to address unfinished learning and acceleration.
Teach, Practice, Apply, and Reflect

SERVING EDUCATIONAL EQUITY

Course 1: Soup
(How do I view and practice equity?)
Address self-awareness, educator bias and build relationships with students.

Course 3: Salad
(How do I ensure student voice and agency?)
Plan consistent opportunities to see, listen, and build on students' strengths while elevating their voices.

Course 2: Appetizer
(How do I examine data and curriculum for equity?)
Use data, survey the curriculum and instructional approaches for equity.

CHAPTER FOUR

- Addresses seeing students, listening to them, and building on their strengths from an assets-based perspective.
- Explore ways educators can use students' diverse experiences to elevate their voice, analogous to the salad stage of meal-planning to accelerate learning.
- Offers strategies for students to own their learning and share perspectives.
- Outlines actionable steps to ensure student agency.

SEEING, LISTENING, AND BUILDING ON STUDENTS' STRENGTHS

The chef prepares the salad with nutritious ingredients, each having a unique role and contribution to making the salad flavorful. The salad is analogous to student voice and agency. Student's voice allows students to share their opinions and ideas, while student agency allows them to take ownership of their learning. Throughout our work with teachers and students, we have supported the ideas, suggestions, and comments that students have shared with us as we have helped them achieve academic success. Using a multi-course analogy, we focus on the importance of ensuring student voice and agency as our salad course; see Figure 4.1.

This chapter allows us to embrace the *SoLD* principle of *Social and Emotional Development*. We believe that students can learn the skills, habits, and mindsets that enable them to self-regulate and develop interpersonal skills, perseverance, and resilience when we provide educational and restorative behavioral support. We agree that children can construct knowledge by connecting what they know to what they are learning within their cultural context. Likewise, we honor their voices and experiences because our students' perceptions of their own abilities influence their learning.

The Where to Begin stage (Figure 4.2) in this chapter supports students to reach their full potential by highlighting the importance of educators seeing the potential of every child, learning about their interests, elevating their voices, and creating learning environments that allow students to thrive. In the following scenario, we present an example of the importance of students sharing their insights as a part of their own motivation for learning.

Story From the Field #7
Sonya's Story

It was 2012, and I was the principal of a large urban school. A troubling phenomenon was brewing at my school and in school communities across the country. I wanted to know why black boys were underperforming compared to other demographics. This trend was the same across suburban and urban communities. I sought to determine if teacher perceptions and expectations played a role in student outcomes. In my 2014 published research study, I hypothesized that making time for culturally relevant instruction and student voice through engagement with text would improve students' reading skills at the fourth- and fifth-grade level. My study would explore and honor the voices of African American male students as they shared their perceptions on factors that promoted or hindered their academic success. The study incorporated perceptions and culturally responsive teaching practices because their voices on the issue were crucial (Boykin & Bailey, 2000). The findings indicated that interests and reading performance improved when students were provided with high-interest, culturally relevant reading materials. Through their open-ended comments, these students explained how important it was to allow them to share their insights, opinions, and commentary on materials used in the classroom.

One statement that resonated explicitly with me many years later was when the student said, "I loved the book because my teacher loved the book." Another student exclaimed, "I wanted to read the book because my teacher made me laugh when she read it, and the boy had similar things happen in his life." Despite the study's focus on fourth- and fifth-grade African American students, I believe the study provided significant implications for educators to ensure equitable instruction for all students. I concluded that teacher perceptions and their ability to elevate students' voices would be essential in student motivation and excitement for learning.

Students' Experiences in Accelerating Their Learning

No matter how many resources educators have in their school libraries and classrooms, they will still need to connect those resources to their students' personal experiences and voices. This connection between learning resources and students' experiences will take teaching and learning to the next level. Inevitably, strategies to assist students in taking agency and purposeful initiative can help them to act with purpose and to achieve the conditions important for success in their own lives.

Addressing unfinished learning and teaching that builds student skills will require educators to tap into ways to motivate students. We contend that selecting

Figure 4.2 • *Where to Begin? Support Students to Reach Their Full Potential*

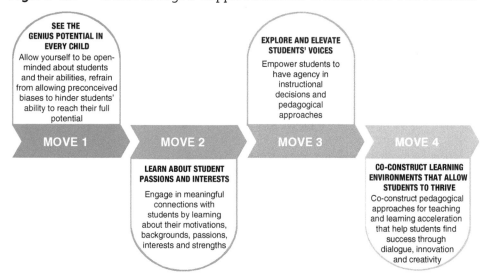

materials that interest students can help them comprehend better, activating prior knowledge and relevance in ways that this goal could not have been achieved otherwise. Demetriou (2019) reminds us that listening to students' voices and encouraging them to share their ideas benefits students' sense of self as learners, and their learning improves along with their self-esteem, self-respect, and relationships with other students as with their teachers. We reflect on the frequency of these interactions in schools and classrooms, connecting educator effectiveness to students' voices. Through quality teaching and learning experiences, educators can allow students to take the driver's seat of their lives using voice and choice. Every child can feel valued if educators evaluate their beliefs and perceptions to determine students' capabilities.

Findings from research guide our own understanding of a student's voice. First, students offer a unique insider's perspective of school culture and climate, and because of this, educators can learn more about how to effectively promote student learning (Bland, 2012). Second, students can share what constraints or promotes their own abilities to succeed or even what supports and hinders their abilities (Caruthers & Friend, 2016). Third, typically in schools, adults decide when, how, and what students can communicate and the extent to which students' views and opinions are sought, considered, or even incorporated into the teaching and learning process (Gillett-Swan & Sargeant, 2018). Fourth, when students (especially those with special needs or disabilities) are not allowed to express themselves when they have been "marginalized because of their disabilities," these students may choose to resist attempts to help with their learning, become alienated from school, and even disconnect from school altogether (Pazey, 2020). Fifth, incorporating and honoring students' voices give students a stronger sense of positive association with the school, a stronger sense of self-worth, a stronger sense of themselves as learners, and a stronger connection to the learning process (Demetriou, 2019). Sixth, students who are not succeeding under the existing classroom conditions are some of the most important voices that need to be heard (Mitra, 2009). Educators who want to promote equity and advance student learning must embrace the opinions, ideas, and viewpoints of all the students in their classrooms.

Story From the Field #8
Gwen's Story

The Elementary School/University Literacy Partnership: Educators make assumptions about students when they do not appreciate the richness of the lived experiences of students. During our partnership, my university teachers-in-training worked with many students in Sonya's central city school. Initially, these novice teachers would serve as literacy tutors who assisted the elementary students with reading and writing assignments. At the beginning of this experience, our novice teachers reflected on the environment surrounding the school and the fact that most had never traveled to this section of town. They honestly expressed their own trepidation about completing this field experience in an urban core school and their own preconceived notions about children in urban core settings. They readily shared that they expected these children to have behavioral problems and extremely poor academic skills; they also shared that they viewed these children as members of a group (high poverty) instead of as individual learners. As they observed classroom practices, student behaviors, and toured the school facility, many expressed surprise that what is considered "normal school practices" were occurring in a pleasant, positive learning environment. None of these novice teachers had lived or worked in the urban core environment. None had engaged in conversations or activities with students whose background, ethnicity, or language had differed from their own. They had preconceived notions and ideas about these students, and how they had assumed that because of the school's location, all the students would be viewed from a deficit lens. They indicated that as new teachers they had not thought about the individuality and uniqueness of each child in a classroom. Nor had they explored how important it was to allow students to express their opinions, share their insights, or collaborate on learning activities. Additionally, these novice teachers indicated that they had never thought about how they would be perceived by the students or how their own behaviors and actions would be examined by these students.

Sonya and I engaged novice teachers and students in several community building activities in which they would get to know each other, establish working parameters, and collaboratively plan their sessions. We used inventories and surveys to determine students' interests in topics, stories, and activities. Over the course of several weeks, the novice teachers and elementary students worked on classroom assignments, participated in collaborative reading and book sharing, and engaged in several writing activities. During the writing activities, we decided to have students create their own narratives based on their interests and experiences. Students created poetry, stories that included fantasy, humor, autobiographies, horror, and adventure, and produced short graphic stories. As the novice teachers listened to the children's descriptions, insights, and commentary, several indicated how surprised they were that the students shared many ideas that were universal themes in childhood. It was obvious that these teachers were not accustomed to exchanging ideas with children nor listening to their lived experiences. The elementary students were encouraged to provide insight, opinions, and commentary throughout the sessions. Initially, many teachers believed they were there to help the "children with deficits" from marginalized communities. Many explained that they had not reflected on how important honoring and acknowledging the children's voices were in promoting self-esteem, learning confidence, and learning efforts. By the time their field experience ended, these teachers and the children with whom they worked had learned to listen and honor the voices of others. At the end of the program, Sonya created a school-wide assembly so that the children could share their published stories, engage in book talks, and display their graphic stories with their families and other children. The novice teachers learned to listen to and respect the voices of individual children rather than make broad assumptions about children based on their zip code. Their perceptions changed drastically, and many wanted to later work at Sonya's school.

> Student voice refers to the expression of values, opinions, beliefs, and perspectives of individuals and groups of students in a school and to instructional approaches and techniques based on student choices, interests, passions, and ambitions. Listening to and acting on student preferences, interests, and perspectives helps students feel invested in their own learning and can ignite passions that will increase their persistence.
> —St. John Briel (2017)

These perceptions become crystallized based on mental models about marginalized students of color. Delpit (1988) asserts that teacher perceptions fail to highlight the individuality and uniqueness of some students in their classrooms. According to Delpit (1999), an important yet typically avoided discussion on power imbalances in the larger U.S. society reverberates in society and classrooms. In her book, *Multiplication Is for White People: Raising Expectations for Other People's Children*, she makes the case that African American students do not achieve their full potential when teachers fail to see their worth. Everyday interactions and assumptions are made about the capacities and integrity of teachers of low-income people of color (Delpit, 2012).

Stop and Reflect

1. What activities do you engage in that celebrate your own students' voices?

2. Do you acknowledge the uniqueness and talents of each of your own students?

Teachers who want to celebrate their own students' voices can start by allowing students to participate in Turn and Talks, Gallery Walks, Round Robin Ideas, and Short Discussions on topics of interest such as favorite books or characters. We believe in starting each class session with the "Good News of the Day." During the first two to three minutes of class, students are encouraged to share key ideas about their lives beyond the classroom or a positive message about an event. Teachers have to plan for this time. Teachers can also have students share entry and exit slips on what they are learning in class. When students have a say in classroom work, their work is more meaningful.

Stop and Reflect

1. What are your perceptions about the students who are in your classroom?

2. How have you offered culturally relevant instruction in your own classroom?

Chapter 4 is analogous to the salad course in the quest for equitable learning environments. The ingredients for the salad typically include vegetables such as tomatoes, lettuce, and onions, proteins such as cheese or nuts, and a salad dressing to finish the dish. Each ingredient has a role and contribution to making the salad flavorful. Educators wishing to accelerate student learning will want to take a similar approach in their school or classroom, recognizing and building on the strengths of every student for optimal teaching and learning that serves every child. Listening to and including students' voices, opinions, and ideas in classroom practices, learning activities, and school policies ensure that their ideas are valued.

In this chapter, we embraced the *SoLD Principle of the Supportive Environment* in which all students engage in strong attachments and relationships as they become a part of the classroom learning community. The classroom is a safe environment for them to share their opinions, ideas, and interests. Students experience trust, encouragement, and respect from classmates and teachers.

Accelerating student learning can be enhanced when teachers understand and embrace them while helping students feel seen and heard. How might educators examine students' perceptions to help them feel seen, heard, and valued while raising their individuality and learning potential? Educators can start acknowledging the importance of a student's voice, provide opportunities for students to share their insights, and use their opinions, views, and insights to enhance learning experiences (Figure 4.3).

Figure 4.3 • SoLD Principles of Practices

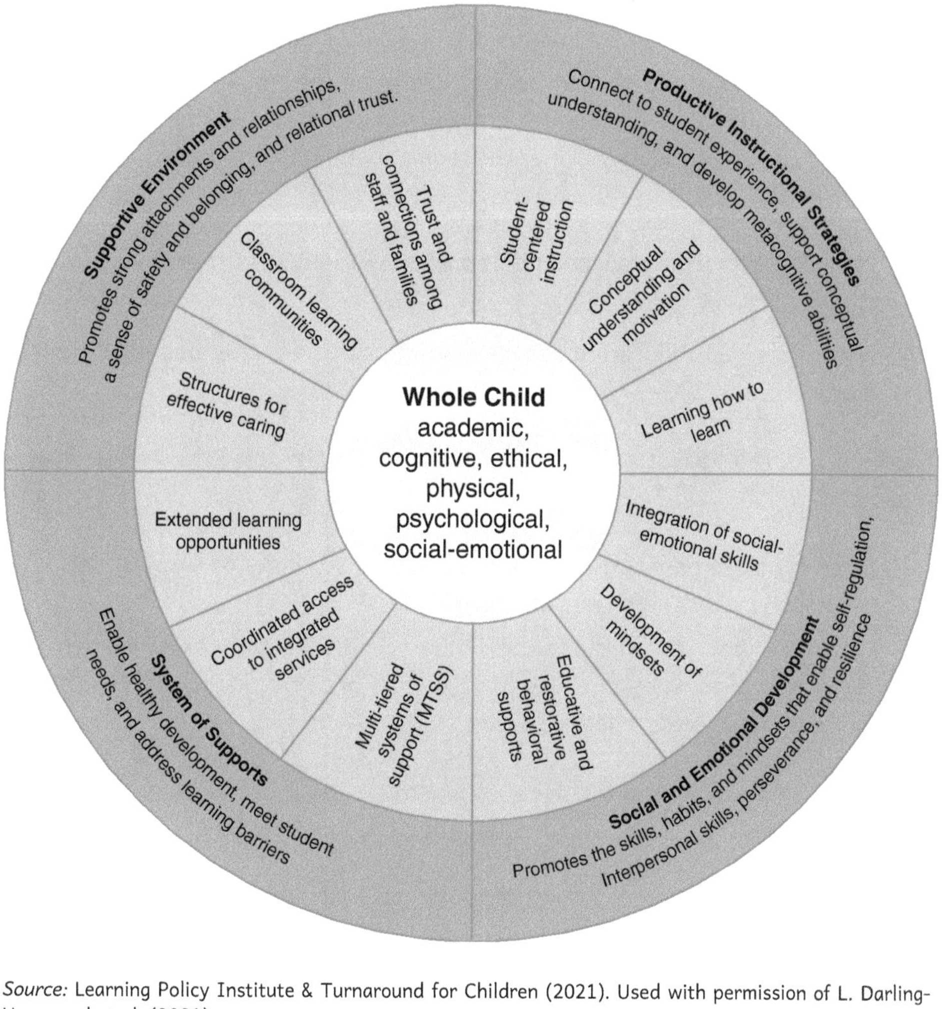

Source: Learning Policy Institute & Turnaround for Children (2021). Used with permission of L. Darling-Hammond et al. (2021).

ELEVATING STUDENT VOICE

How Do We Elevate the Voices of the Students We Serve?

> When adults consult with students and afford them the space and opportunity to share their perspectives and insights in terms of how they learn and wish to be regarded and supported by others, students gain the sense their voices matter.
> —Pazey (2021)

In Story From the Field #8, the novice teachers elevated students' voices through the use of inventories, information exchanges, informal discussions, and surveys to determine the topics, stories, and activities that were of interest to the elementary students. We incorporated student journalism, book talks, idea exchanges, and Gallery Walks as the major vehicles for sharing. To ensure that all students and especially those students with disabilities are included and are encouraged to share their ideas, educators are encouraged to

1. Provide children the space and opportunity to express their views.
2. Facilitate their ability to express their views.
3. Listen to what children have to say, and as appropriate, act upon their views (Lundy, 2007).

The following self-reflecting questions can guide in elevating the voices of all students:

1. Does my classroom provide a safe space for students to express their opinions without judgment or reprisals?
2. When and how do I provide the venue or learning activity for honest, open-idea exchanges in which my students are not judged on how they express their lived experiences?

Pazey (2021) captured the following comments made by children with disabilities when they were asked about their own experiences.

- "Don't look at a student and then just make an assumption about that student. Take time to really get to know the student, even if the student is rough around the edges."

- "Whoever is in charge should always make sure that the students come first, that the students have a place to work, the students are encouraged to work, and that teachers do not give up."
- "She cares enough about what you need and what you think is important."

Elevating the voices of students has to be inclusive, and this is especially true for students with disabilities. Too often in our classrooms, many children are ignored, had decisions made for them, or are treated as though their opinions did not matter (Fletcher, 2015; Hajdukova et al., 2016).

Stop and Reflect

In what ways do you ensure that your students with disabilities and special needs are included in all instructional activities and learning events?

Teachers can use the following activities to elevate students' voices:

1. Provide time for information exchanges within the class.
2. Utilize students' "All About Me" sessions to encourage students to share important events during small group exchanges.
3. Engage students in decision-making concerning classroom rules and practices.
4. Ensure that students give their opinions, ideas, and commentary on school-wide practices such as school mascots, insignias, colors, and sports.
5. Invite student input on materials and resources to include in both classroom and school libraries. Students can vote on selections, and offer elevator pitches on why certain books/stories should be included.
6. Promote student podcasts and short video clips of current school events.
7. Spotlight students' stories, poetry, and writing.
8. Create a classroom climate that encourages diverse views and a safe place to share.

Getting Up Close and Personal Reflective Questions

Educators should ask the following questions:

- Am I providing experiences that allow students to bring their authentic experiences?

- Do I regularly give all students the opportunity to express themselves or contribute to class discussions?

Take Action

Now that you have explored mindset, perceptions, and steps to take to serve students' educational equity, act on your learning by completing the following application.

Read, Respond, and Reflect

Read the Stories From the Field again and think about the comments:

- "I loved the book because my teacher loved the book."
- "I wanted to read the book because my teacher read it and made me laugh."
- "They had not thought about the individuality and uniqueness of each child in a classroom."
- "Nor had they explored how important it was to allow students an opportunity to express their opinions, share their insights, or collaborate on learning activities."

Let's Reflect

- Do you intentionally encourage student voices in your classroom?
- Is student voice and agency talked about in your collaborative team meetings?
- Do current professional learning opportunities promote student voice and agency?

Respond

- It is "easy" to misinterpret student capabilities if we do not hear what they are saying. Do you agree or disagree? Why or why not?
- Whose voices are usually heard? Why?
- Whose voices are potentially looked over? Why?

SUMMARY

Being intentional about recognizing a student's voice means examining one's current instructional practices and implementing the necessary changes in classroom climate and structure so that the diverse voices of all students are recognized. Educators can use surveys, informal discussions, interest inventories, and idea exchanges to encourage students to share their own ideas, opinions, and commentaries. We have learned that the opinions of all students are important, and classroom teachers must actively seek to include students with disabilities in all discussions, idea exchanges, and classroom decisions. Educators must create a classroom environment in which students are encouraged to share with peers. Students learn to take ownership of their learning when their ideas, opinions, and voices are respected and encouraged.

TIME TO DIG IN TOOLS

Activity	Description	Research Support and Reference	Link
Identify Safe Classrooms: Places to Belong and Learn	This website includes activities, practices, and resources for creating identity-safe classrooms.	Dorothy M. Steele and Becki Cohn-Vargas Cohn-Vargas, B., Kahn, A.C., Epstein, A., & Gogolewski, K. (2021). *Belonging and inclusion in identity-safe schools*. Thousand Oaks, CA: Corwin.	http://www. identitysafe classrooms. com/
Administer surveys to honor student voices and ideas about their perceptions of teacher expectations	Panorama Education Student Survey	In August 2014, researchers at the Harvard Graduate School of Education and Panorama Education launched a first-of-its-kind collaboration to develop a valid and reliable survey tool to measure student perceptions of teaching and learning.	https://www. panoramaed. com/ panorama-student-survey
The Power of Affirming One's Values: Classrooms as Supporting Spaces	This website provides values affirmation activities that can be easily implemented in fifteen minutes or less with students.	Northeastern Center for Advancing Teaching and Learning Through Research	https:// qrs.ly/9qeqdyl

Activity	Description	Research Support and Reference	Link
Implement co-teaching opportunities with students to elevate their voice and agency.	Students are finding their own voice and improving their communication skills.	Adjapong, E. S., & Emdin, C. (2015). Rethinking pedagogy in urban spaces: Implementing Hip-Hop pedagogy in the urban science classroom. *Journal of Urban Learning Teaching and Research, 11*, 66–77. https://files.eric.ed.gov/fulltext/EJ1071416.pdf	Hip Hop Pedagogical Practices https://qrs.ly/vverq6a https://qrs.ly/ojeqdxz
"Warm demander" teachers expect great things from students, convince them of their own brilliance, and help students reach their potential in a disciplined, structured environment (Alexander, 2016)	Expectations of teachers	Alexander, M. (2016, April 13). The warm demander: An equity approach. Edutopia. https://www.edutopia.org/blog/warm-demander-equity-approach-matt-alexander	Warm Demander (Look, See, Warm Demander – Look, Feel, Sound ChartFeel, Chart) https://qrs.ly/6heqdyc
Gallery Walks	Discussion technique in which students share insights as they examine exhibits, written selections, or posted comments while visiting stations around the classroom.	Nurani, A. D. K. S., & Rukmini, D. (2017). Gallery walk and think-pair-share techniques for teaching writing descriptive text to students with high and low motivation. *English Education Journal, 7*(3), 206–212.	https://qrs.ly/18eqdyr

(Continued)

(Continued)

Activity	Description	Research Support and Reference	Link
Empower student voice and leadership in school life and education issues	Create structures (surveys to gather many student voices about the school climate): Use brainstorming, debates, voting, polls, student-led conferences, and appropriate social media such as class blogs.	Snelling, J. (2018). 8 ways to empower student voices in your classroom. https://www.iste.org/explore/In-the-classroom/8-ways-to-empower-student-voice-in-your-classroom	https://qrs.ly/31eqdyu
Promote student voice, engagement, leadership and connections between students	Create opportunities for sharing student and staff narratives; create opportunities for students to share and speak with students and staff.	AMSD. (2018). Reimagine Minnesota: Equity and education for All. https://www.amsd.org/wp-content/uploads/2019/01/ReimagineMinnesotaOverview121118.final_-1.pdf	https://qrs.ly/g9eqdyw
Culturally Responsive Education Hub	Provides practitioners with an array of resources to advance culturally responsive education and ethnic studies. These include research studies and briefs, resources for culturally responsive education during remote learning, and a video series that illustrate the impact of culturally responsive education	https://crehub.org/	https://crehub.org/

Activity	Description	Research Support and Reference	Link
	from the perspective of educators, parents, and students.		
Culturally Responsive Teaching (Edutopia)	A webpage that provides practitioners with links to articles, resources, and videos that support culturally responsive teaching. The resources cover topics, including broader discussion of how to advance equity and racism in the classroom at various grade levels, as well as guidance on how to adopt and implement a range of discrete culturally responsive teaching practices.	https://www.edutopia.org/topic/culturally-responsive-teaching	https://qrs.ly/bzeqdz0
Not In Our School (Not In Our Town)	This website includes lesson plans, professional development guides, and other resources to support the creation of safe, accepting, and inclusive school communities.	https://www.niot.org/nios	https://www.niot.org/nios

(Continued)

(Continued)

Activity	Description	Research Support and Reference	Link
Culturally Responsive Teaching and the Brain	This book offers an approach for designing and implementing culturally responsive instruction consistent with research on brain development and neuroscience.	Edutopia: https://www.edutopia.org/blog/making-connections-culturally-responsive-teaching-and-brain-elena-aguilar	https://crtandthebrain.com/book/

CHAPTER 5

THE MAIN COURSE

Effective Equitable Instruction

> We can, whenever we choose, successfully teach all children whose schooling is of interest to us. We already know more than we need to do that. Whether or not we do it must finally depend on how we feel about the fact that we haven't so far.
> —Ron Edmonds (1982)

Figure 5.1 • *Murray and Turner's (2021) Five-Course Framework for Accelerated Learning*

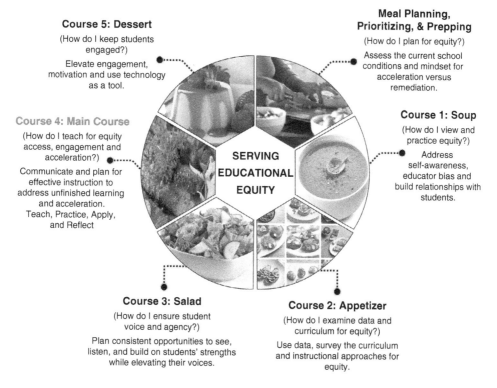

Course 5: Dessert
(How do I keep students engaged?)
Elevate engagement, motivation and use technology as a tool.

Meal Planning, Prioritizing, & Prepping
(How do I plan for equity?)
Assess the current school conditions and mindset for acceleration versus remediation.

Course 4: Main Course
(How do I teach for equity access, engagement and acceleration?)
Communicate and plan for effective instruction to address unfinished learning and acceleration.
Teach, Practice, Apply, and Reflect

SERVING EDUCATIONAL EQUITY

Course 1: Soup
(How do I view and practice equity?)
Address self-awareness, educator bias and build relationships with students.

Course 3: Salad
(How do I ensure student voice and agency?)
Plan consistent opportunities to see, listen, and build on students' strengths while elevating their voices.

Course 2: Appetizer
(How do I examine data and curriculum for equity?)
Use data, survey the curriculum and instructional approaches for equity.

CHAPTER FIVE

- Explores effective instruction that addresses unfinished learning, enhances student engagement, and advances learning.
- Highlights the importance of communication and planning for effective instruction.
- Explores, without teacher bias, the learning needs of students.
- Discusses effective planning, instruction, and lesson execution.
- Provides strategies to scaffold teaching and learning so that the needs of all students are met.
- Discusses equity and students with disabilities.
- Highlights the importance of incorporating equity into instructional practices.

Instructional equity means that every student learns the lesson daily and can demonstrate evidence of their learning; it's not enough that every student has access to the lesson. In other words, just because the teacher is teaching the lesson doesn't mean that every student is learning the lesson (Toth, 2021). In this chapter we use the "main course" as an analogy to teaching that provides access to equity, engagement, and aacceleration; see Figure 5.1.

This chapter allows us to embrace the *SoLD* principle of *Productive Instructional Strategies, which connect to students' experiences, support conceptual understanding, and helps students* develop metacognitive abilities. This principle allows us to embrace student-centered learning, enhance learning motivation, and focus on helping students become less dependent and more independent as they learn how to learn. Author and scholar Zaretta Hammond compares Independent and Dependent learners in Figure 5.2, supporting educators to be reflective in creating environments where all students are supported to grapple with complex texts and tasks (Hammond, 2015). These environments support students, regardless of their cultural and linguistic background, to thrive and engage with rigorous learning experiences.

EFFECTIVE INSTRUCTION THAT ADDRESSES UNFINISHED LEARNING, STUDENT ENGAGEMENT, AND LEARNING ACCELERATION

We have arrived at the main course in our menu analogy. The chef prepares the main dishes or entrées with care and expertise, using the highest quality

Figure 5.2 • *Dependent Learner Characteristics vs. Independent Learner*

The Dependent Learner	The Independent Learner
• Is dependent on the teacher to carry most of the cognitive load of a task always	• Relies on the teacher to carry some of the cognitive load temporarily
• Is unsure of how to tackle a new task	• Utilizes strategies and processes for tackling a new task
• Cannot complete a task without scaffolds	• Regularly attempts new tasks without scaffolds
• Will sit passively and wait if stuck until teacher intervenes	• Has cognitive strategies for getting unstuck
• Doesn't retain information well or "doesn't get it"	• Has learned how to retrieve information from long-term memory

Source: Hammond (2015, p. 14).

ingredients during meal preparation. The entrée is the main course and may include proteins such as meat and vegetables. The entrée requires specific steps from its selection as a menu item, preparation of ingredients, and actual cooking until its final presentation at the meal. We maintain that the entrée is analogous to equitable instruction in that educators communicate and align high expectations for all students while providing appropriate instruction. Explicit instruction promotes productive struggle and enhances metacognition through various experiential learning opportunities. Equitable Instruction (Figure 5.3) is a process that we believe must include these specifics: (a) communicate and align high expectations, (b) assess students' learning needs accurately, (c) employ high-quality curriculum and instruction that engages learners, (d) utilize instruction for grade-level mastery of standards, (e) use instructional scaffolding that promotes metacognition and independent learning, and (f) engage in a cycle of teaching monitoring, assessing, and reflecting.

Communicating High Expectations for Learning Acceleration

> Being able to communicate is vital to being an effective educator. Communication not only conveys information, but it encourages effort, modifies attitudes, and stimulates thinking.
> —Leah Davies (2018)

Figure 5.3 • *Serving Equitable Instruction—Steps to Instructional Recovery and Acceleration*

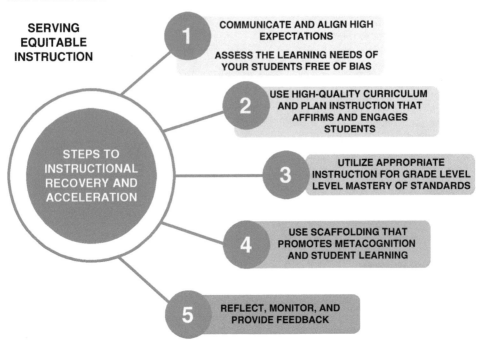

Likewise, we agree with Leah Davies (2018) that effective communication for educators is not only *understanding and acknowledgment; it is agreement and commitment*. High expectations for student learning must be communicated regularly throughout the district, school, and especially in the classroom. Fisher and Frey (2022) conclude that students whose teachers communicate their high expectations and beliefs succeed substantially better than students whose teachers have low expectations. They remind us that educators **can learn** to use high-expectation practices such as

1. Engaging all students in choosing creative and challenging activities.
2. Creating classroom environments that are engaging, caring, and respectful.
3. Helping students set learning goals, monitor progress, and promote student autonomy in their learning.

Therefore, district and school-level leaders must communicate and work together to forge plans that address unfinished learning and teaching. Accordingly, we frame this chapter as the main course. We recommend the

SWOT analysis we suggested in Chapter 1 to start the communication process so that school and district-level leaders align on their critical next steps.

The questions of what to do sequentially and logically could help all stakeholders move forward using a clear pathway that involves teaching, monitoring, reflecting, and reassessing, as outlined in Figure 5.3. An approach that engages and holds students to high standards would need to be embraced to engage students in meaningful learning. A process that elevates accelerated learning could help teachers move from covering content to teaching for mastery.

Stop and Reflect

How do you communicate high expectations for your students? We recommend that you examine your own classroom instructional practices with the High Expectations Self-Assessment Checklist (bit.ly/40DiDMy). Once you have examined your practices, reflect on how you communicate your expectations regularly with students, parents, and other educators.

Assessing Without Bias the Learning Needs of Your Students

> When discussing inequality in the classroom, it's tempting to focus on external factors like socioeconomic status or educational tools like rubrics; it's more uncomfortable to tackle a topic like teacher bias. After all, no one wants to think they are biased, particularly not people who devote their time, money, and energy to teaching the next generation.
> —Marco Learning (2018)

Do you use your students' assessments to make conclusions about them as learners? Too often, we label and judge others based on our preconceived notions. We encourage teachers to use multiple forms of data to assess learning needs. Chapter 2 discussed the importance of formative and summative data sources. As teachers move students forward into their learning recovery, we believe that assessments should be utilized without bias toward students who have been traditionally marginalized. We believe that information about student learning can be assessed using direct measures, such as exams and reports, and indirect measures, such as surveys and interest inventories. We encourage teachers to use formative assessments that measure student learning on an ongoing basis. Lastly, we use informal measures such as exit slips, gallery walks, and book talks to garner learning.

Story From the Field #9

During a recent visit to an urban school in the midwest, we observed an educator preparing students with rituals before engaging in their daily mathematics lesson. Students were asked to recite the quote, "Excuses are the tools of the weak and incompetent used to build monuments of nothingness. Those who excel in it seldom excel in anything else but excuses." – Anonymous

The teacher projected the quotes, and students recited them in unison as they engaged in their mathematics learning for the day. They loudly exclaimed, "Once a task has just begun, never leave it until it's done. Be the labor great or small, do it well or not at all." Afterwards, the teacher reminded them often that she felt they could achieve high expectations, and she tried another strategy, "Three Before Me." (Appendix G) Students were to use their resources, such as reviewing the directions and other tools, to help them succeed, including trying different approaches to solving the task. Secondly, they were to utilize the classroom's instructional real estate (displays, references), such as anchor charts or other visual resources. Finally, they were charged with silently asking a classmate if they were unsure of expectations or for clarification. If these three strategies are unsuccessful, they could ask the teacher.

The interactions between the educator and students were validating and powerful. The mantras provided strong affirmation to the students that the teacher believed in their ability to tackle challenging, grade-level tasks despite their academic ability levels. This teaching example communicated to students that they had the tools to solve all the tasks successfully. It removed the deficit thinking that certain mathematics tasks were impossible and instilled in students the drive to try. Because their teacher believed in their success, these students made a stronger effort. During the visit, it was clear that the educator had formed a strong, trusting relationship with the students, and they would rise to her expectation level. If educators are going to get students to do challenging work, they must encourage their students to grapple with hard tasks. Deficit thinking about students' abilities should be addressed and eliminated.

This interaction exemplified an effective teaching strategy from Doug Lemov's (2021) book, *Teach Like a Champion*, which helps teachers maintain high expectations for every student—even those who don't have high expectations for themselves. Lemov (2021) describes No Opt Out as a sequence that begins with a student unable (or unwilling) to answer a question, the teacher and classmates providing assistance, and ends with that same student giving the correct answer as often as possible, even if it is only to repeat the correct behavior.

Students should be presented with a rich, rigorous, culturally relevant curriculum that fosters critical thinking and problem-solving.

Curriculum and Instruction for Learning Acceleration

We believe that there is an alignment between the content standards, curriculum, instruction, student learning, and assessment needed to address unfinished learning. In Chapter 3, we suggested that educators utilize EdReports.org to evaluate the quality of the curriculum chosen. As you choose lessons within the curriculum, focus on those that allow students to engage in critical thinking and problem-solving. We ask teachers to answer the following questions about their curriculum:

Stop and Reflect

Does your curriculum allow you to do the following?

1. Frequently evaluate and change instruction as needed
2. Provide opportunities for student engagement, critical thinking, and problem-solving
3. Provide various strategies and models that foster innovation and creativity
4. Provide instruction for students at all levels
5. Develop assessments that are reflective of grade-level standards
6. Provide meaningful engagement
7. Collaborate with others across grade levels

Source: Adapted from *Universal Instructional Design Checklist* (Myers, 2016).

Story From the Field #10

During a recent planning meeting with district and school-level leaders, we overheard a district administrator and building-level leader discuss the performance of the building leader's school. The district administrator insisted that the school needed to use the existing curriculum. The building leader expressed frustration with the curriculum, loss of teaching staff, student absenteeism, and overall gaps in student learning that causes performance to decline. The conversation was intense, with both leaders communicating their positions. The school leader wished to support the wishes of his staff to return students to "basic skills" as a remedy for student learning loss. The building leader contended, *"Our teachers are frustrated that some students are not where they need to be academically. The curriculum is above students' heads. For example, we have seventh and eighth-grade students reading at the third-grade level. These kids need to go back to the basics."*

District officials were mandating the established curriculum and pacing. During the conversation, it became clear that the two educators were passionate about their positions and would not be able to solve the problems until they engaged in a dialogue that focused on mutual understanding and sharing of information.

This scenario in Story From the Field #10 provides an excellent example of what we have experienced in schools, specifically when there is a need for clear communication about systems, structures, and learning goals. We have witnessed too many times when educators, with the best intentions, did not engage in meaningful communication as they sought answers to their instructional recovery. We believe that acceleration starts when the stakeholders have clear lines of communication during which high expectations are shared, learning goals and the curriculum are aligned, and instruction focuses on acceleration, not remediation.

Start With Intellectually Prepared Lessons

How do you prepare for your lessons? As we examine learning loss and the struggles that both teachers and students face, preparing for the various needs of students has never been more important. High-performing schools have termed this focus "intellectual preparation." Intellectual Preparation allows teachers to create, revise, and internalize high-quality lessons before delivering them to students to ensure all students can succeed with rigorous instruction (Kennedy, 2019). We believe teachers can best plan to support students of varying backgrounds by engaging in intellectual preparation and planning as Matthew Joseph (2020) outlined:

- *Anticipate what students might struggle with during a lesson and prepare.*
- *Give students time to struggle with tasks and ask questions.*
- *Build a culture where confusion and mistakes are part of learning.*
- *Praise students for their efforts.*
- *Help students realize this struggle will take time.*
- *Provide strategies for what they can do when they are stuck.*

Teachers can alter existing lessons to ensure that they include equitable opportunities for the productive struggle, free of educator bias. See the sample lessons in Appendix B and C for math and language arts lessons. We believe that lessons can focus on helping all students master content and engage them in critical thinking and problem-solving.

Specific strategies that we have found to be effective include chunking portions of the lesson and zeroing in on the most important priority learning . All students deserve access, even if the material is challenging.

Lesson Preparation

Teachers we have supported take the following steps to intellectually prepare:

Step 1: Understand the big idea/concept at play in the lesson.

Step 2: Do the core tasks of the lesson to develop/refine exemplary student responses that can help students better set up for success.

Step 3: Anticipate student misconceptions and create questions/supports to address these misconceptions.

Step 4: As necessary/appropriate, adjust the plan to ensure student success.

Focus on Grade Level Work

Responding to the Question: Should I ever use remediation?

We believe that the instructional focus should be on grade-level work. Therefore, we want to address critical questions we hear from educators. For example, "If productive struggle and core readiness are the goals, should I ever remediate student learning?" and "How can I ensure students master core math and literacy skills when they need help?" We respond that we want to offer students the instruction they need in *real-time* and build on their strengths rather than focusing on deficits as remediation has traditionally done. We must provide students access to grade-level materials to prepare them for college and careers. Furthermore, we do students a disservice when we do not design instruction that advances their learning. For example, when we consistently have students use below-grade-level materials and do not allow them to engage in critical reflection, we do not allow them to access their full potential. Therefore, we believe that teachers can begin with a mindset shift from "*How will I ever catch students up who are so behind academically?*" to "*Are we providing the instruction that students need to advance their learning?*"

Appropriate Instruction for Mastery

> **Effective instruction involves a dynamic interplay among content to be learned, pedagogical methods applied, characteristics of individual learners, and the context in which the learning occurs.**
> —H. D. Schalock (1993)

How do you offer effective instruction? Effective teaching connects to students' experiences, engages students in active learning, supports their conceptual understanding and motivation, and helps develop metacognitive abilities so that students learn how to learn. We embrace effective and productive instructional strategies and approaches as significant components of the *SoLD* principles (Darling-Hammond et al., 2020). In our experiences, effective instruction means that we, as teachers, use a variety of approaches such as scaffolding, direct instruction, indirect instruction, interactive learning, and experiential learning to meet students' just-in-time learning. We engage in helping students develop metacognitive tools such as text analysis, context clues, and problem-solution sequences that help them *learn-how-to-learn* on their own. In addition, we support the need for additional time for learning, scaffolding for new learning, and intensive tutoring to assist students. We have discovered that multiple methods of instruction allow for various means of student engagement and various responses to indicate learning. H. D. Schalock (1993) reminds us, "*No single instructional strategy can be used in all situations; instead, various approaches have to be used because of students' varying abilities, experiences, and interests.*"

Story From the Field #11

In a recent conversation with new and veteran teachers, we brainstormed opportunities to focus on "grade-level instruction" when students have gaps in their learning. Teachers posed the following questions and comments: "How do we focus on grade-level core expectations when students are experiencing severe math and reading challenges due to intermittent schooling?" For example, one of the teachers shared, "The strategies I implemented previously to combat learning loss are simply not working, and some of my students stare blankly at me when I introduce concepts. I know the words 'learning loss' are not acceptable in these times, but what suggestions do you have for me to help students find success who truly are struggling?" Another commented, "About a fourth of my students are reading below grade level, and their challenges have exacerbated since returning to school." One frustrated teacher commented, "I am concerned about my students with special education needs who would benefit from staying in class; however, I do not believe I am being successful. What can I do to ensure that I am meeting the needs of these students?" Finally, a teacher asked, "What instruction can be offered to ensure learning for my students?"

What the teachers experienced in Story From the Field #11 were challenges associated with giving students access to a grade-level curriculum and experiential learning experiences when the students are not yet ready to tackle the work independently. We realized that these teachers needed to provide instruction that resulted in student learning. Also, their students needed tools for guided and independent learning and metacognitive success, just as a chef needs tools and proper food preparation and service equipment to prepare a successful meal. The tools can be implemented through careful planning using *just-in-time* approaches to instructional recovery.

We encourage you to reflect on your instructional practices as you seek to advance your students' learning. Teachers who want to provide constructive, practical, and meaningful instruction are encouraged to ask themselves the following questions:

Stop and Reflect

1. Is the instruction culturally relevant?

2. Does this teaching approach address my students' needs within learning outcomes and objectives?

3. Will the instructional approach provide guided and independent practice within a meaningful context?

4. Does this instructional approach allow explaining examples, modeling strategies, classifying concepts, and demonstrating tasks?

5. Does this instructional approach engage my students in active learning across multiple means?

6. Will my students be able to use what is being taught across disciplines?

7. Will this approach garner various responses to indicate student learning?

We believe that if a disconnect exists between what is being taught and what students are to master, teachers and students will experience the frustrations that the teachers in Story From the Field #11 discussed. Therefore, instructional recovery focuses on prioritizing critical prerequisite skills and knowledge and helping students connect with new learning.

We support multiple modes of instruction to ensure equity in classroom instruction: Direct Instruction, Interactive Instruction, Indirect Instruction, Experiential Learning, and Independent Learning. Implementing direct instruction means the teacher provides explicit instruction, modeling, scaffolding, and guidance. We use various resources to reach our students, including videos and demonstrations. We employ indirect instruction, which is student-centered and includes debates, case studies, student projects, and problem-solving activities. Furthermore, we have found that experiential learning, such as field trips, experiments, games, and observations, helps students engage in hands-on, action-based learning activities. We use interactive instruction to engage students in discussions, debates, group projects, and brainstorming as they problem-solve. Additionally, we promote independent learning for students to engage in research, homework practice, and application activities. Teachers who want to embrace these multiple modes of instruction can find additional examples in Appendix A: Instructional Approaches for Equitable Practices.

Teachers are the drivers of teaching and learning and can offer the most effective approach based on student's learning abilities and needs. We firmly assert that the best approach to learning recovery allows students to take on more of the cognitive lift, celebrating opportunities for productively struggling and having students take ownership of their learning.

Story From the Field #12

Working with students at various levels, we noticed that learning could be debilitating for students. We have heard these comments from students: "If I can't find the answer immediately, I just give up." "I didn't know what to do. I am frustrated and I don't know how to do this work!" These comments define destructive struggle, which occurs when students become disengaged, overwhelmed, and frustrated with their ability and efforts. Some students will cry or become highly disruptive to the learning environment. They feel like failures, and that success is not within their reach. These students have lost confidence in their ability to try.

We have also heard sentiments from students and teachers, such as. "I have an idea! Let's try this." "I just haven't gotten this yet! But it's on the tip of my tongue. Can I do it this way?"

In contrast, productive struggle celebrates the messiness of learning, allows students to make mistakes, and celebrates their effort but doesn't give false hope. Learning takes time, and students are proud when they finally get it. There is a willingness to keep trying, persist, and stay engaged while trying to learn. Intermediate progress and insight are possible to students even if completion or the correct answer has not been reached. There is learning in exploring how best to improve learning and a strong belief that students can achieve if they try.

Story From the Field #12 reminds us that learning takes time and requires great investment for both students and teachers. We contend that teachers will want to embrace opportunities for students to engage in productive struggle to support students' mathematical and literacy skills. Marcella Bullmaster-Day (2021) states that productive struggle is "*Effortful practice that goes beyond passive reading, listening, or watching—that builds useful, lasting understanding and skill.*" We support Bullmaster-Day's (2021) conclusion *that* academic struggle is not productive when students do not understand the learning goal, feel unsafe to fail, or do not receive adequate and appropriate support. We believe that students who engage in productive struggle get a chance to learn from their mistakes and strengthen their learning. We have found that through productive struggle, students engage in metacognitive strategies when they practice, receive feedback, and use their critical thinking to solve problems or seek solutions.

Author and researcher Zaretta Hammond (2015) encourages educators to foster productive struggle by communicating personal warmth toward students while simultaneously demanding they work toward high standards. *The Ready for Rigor* framework (Zaretta Hammond, 2013) codifies four core areas we must synthesize and braid together to help students become leaders in their learning. These areas are awareness, learning partnerships, information processing capacity, and learning communities and environments. We encourage educators to examine their instructional practices to ensure they prepare students for the rigor as Zaretta Hammond outlines in her framework; see Appendix D.

Stop and Reflect

1. How do you provide opportunities for your students to make mistakes?

2. Do you model and embrace a culture where students learn from their mistakes?

3. Are students able to tackle challenging content on their own?

4. Who does most of the talking in your classroom?

5. Is there a culture of error that allows students to make mistakes and learn with and from one another?

Scaffolding That Promotes Metacognition and Student Learning

How do you plan to engage your own students in challenging text? All students need access to text, even challenging or complex text, and the way to grant that access is through scaffolding. Scaffolding offers support and guidance to help students tackle challenging text (Askell-Williams et al., 2012; Palinscar, 1986). We believe that scaffolding starts with teachers planning how-to guide, monitor, and support students as they process complex text. Teachers examine the text and determine what will make it difficult for students, such as the vocabulary or concepts presented. For example, if the text has complex language, the teacher helps the students define and discuss the words *before* reading. If the text deals with concepts or topics new to students, the teachers use advanced organizers to connect what students already know to further information or help them make predictions and ask questions to guide them through the new topics. When students lack the fluency to master the text, the student listens to the text being read, and they engage in paired reading, echo reading, and repeated readings to develop both their own fluency and comprehension. Students do not progress in literacy development when they are not allowed to read grade-level text or complex text. Instead of remediation, which tends to focus on the teaching and learning of isolated reading skills, we propose that teachers allow students to stretch their literacy abilities by supporting their efforts through *close* reading, which helps students learn how to analyze text. This helps them to identify as readers and writers.

In Story From the Field #12 it was obvious that students needed to be taught how to analyze the text, engage in pre-during-post reading events, and reflect on the key points. The instruction provided started with direct, explicit support and then engaged students in their own discussions and reflective inquiries. We believe that several instructional strategies and activities can positively influence equity in literacy instruction while advancing students' literacy abilities. We offer examples in Appendix A. These research-based instructional strategies allow for active engagement, personal reflection, and critical thinking.

Story From the Field #13

During one of our recent school visits to a large urban district, we observed the implementation of several new programs. The school's leader was proud of the multiple initiatives and "bells and whistles" programs she garnered to improve student achievement. Unfortunately, these programs were suggested as best practices instead of a solid, steady plan for measurable gains. In too many schools, we see students inundated with these programs, ignoring the science and best practice opportunities, often leaving students to spend considerable periods on assisted technology without the proper guidance or direct teaching from a teacher. We noticed during our school visits that educators did not utilize data to predict appropriate courses of action.

As we reflect on the best approach to equitable instructional practice, allowing teachers enough time to become familiar with methods and materials is the most effective way. Many school educators use previously utilized programs without connecting the success of those programs to student impact, or they implement programs looking for a quick fix (Gellert, 2022). There are no quick fixes. The calculated process of engaging in meaningful professional learning for teachers, open communication, and common expectations between stakeholders coupled with a specific focus on strategies and structures can help leaders determine what, why, and how instructional recovery is taking place that leads to student impact.

Equity and Students With Disabilities

> To create an inclusive classroom where all students are respected, it is important to use language that prioritizes the student over his or her disability. Disability labels can stigmatize and perpetuate false stereotypes that students who are disabled are not as capable as their peers.
> —Danielle Picard (2022)

We believe that students with disabilities face unique challenges in the classroom. Too often, they are viewed by the labels and categories of their disabilities instead of being seen as active, vibrant community members with unique interests, personalities, and skill sets (Hotez, 2021).

Barbara Blackburn (2017) reminds us that children with special needs are expected to meet their grade-level standards and should be taught with rigorous instruction. Furthermore, Blackburn (2017) identifies three strategies that can be implemented in classrooms to support students with special needs. First, we need to help these students learn by modeling, offering cues, and facilitating problem-solving to become more independent. Children with special needs can learn and meet high expectations when given appropriate support. Many students engage in learned helplessness and seek help from others even when they know the answers. We must recognize that some children with special needs will engage in dependent learning behaviors. Second, children with special needs need appropriate scaffolding and modeling for specific learning tasks, such as answering higher-ordered questions. Having high expectations without offering the appropriate support leads many children to frustration and failure. Third, raising the level of support based on the learning task helps to engage students in problem-solving. Teachers can guide students through an understanding of complex text and tasks.

We believe that students with disabilities need multiple means of representation, action and expression, and engagement to excel academically (Ralabate, 2011;

Spooner et al., 2007). In our work with students who have disabilities, we have embraced the following key concepts: (a) maintain structure; therefore, we need to keep the classroom organized to reduce stress and distractions; (b) break tasks into small, manageable steps, emphasize key points, and keep instructions and choices clear; (c) keep lines of communication open between general education teacher, special education teacher, parents, and child; (d) provide opportunities for success for students who need to experience growth; (e) provide oral, written, and recorded instructions; (f) provide specific feedback and specific praise, and help students correct their own mistakes; (g) provide frequent progress checks; (h) use concrete examples and utilize multimedia materials; and (i) review accommodations/modifications/recommendations provided for each student. Students who are engaged in online learning will also need the following: (j) individual and small-group breakout rooms for support and encouragement; (k) advanced organizers to summarize the order of activities; (l) active use of assistive technology; and (m) stress-reducing activities. Gwen uses relaxing music and yoga videos that students can review to help them create their own "calm zone" for learning (Branstetter, 2020).

Instruction for Students With Disabilities

Targeted interventions for students with Individualized Education Plans (IEPs) should not occur at the expense of their also receiving high-quality grade-level instruction with the remainder of the class. As much as possible, students should receive high-quality grade-level instruction, especially in English Language Arts, where they can develop an academic vocabulary that is vital to their literary success. We have witnessed students with IEPs thrive best when supported in mainstream settings through co-teaching or models with an extra teacher or paraprofessional supporting their learning in the core classroom. Educators can consider supporting all students using the Tiered Intervention Model (Figure 5.4).

Stop and Reflect

1. How do you ensure equity in your classroom for all students, including those with disabilities?

2. Are student IEP goals written to support their success in the regular classroom?

3. When removed from your classroom for resource and pull-out instruction, are the learning goals the same as what they would receive in the core classroom? Why or why not?

Figure 5.4 • *Tiered Intervention Model*

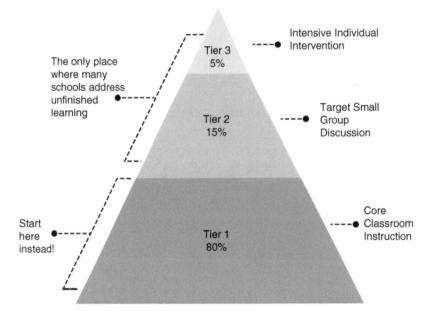

We have discovered that one of the most effective methods for ensuring equity in the classroom for students with and without disabilities has been to incorporate the Universal Design for Learning (UDL) framework (Meyer et al., 2014). The UDL framework fits seamlessly into our **SoLD** Principles of *Productive Instructional Strategies* and a *Supportive Environment*. We support this framework because it provides suggestions that can be applied to any discipline, and its purpose is to ensure that all learners can access and participate in meaningful, challenging learning activities (Figure 5.5).

The major focus is on educators developing lessons and learning experiences that allow all students' engagement, representation, action, and expression. As teachers are planning lessons, they reflect on how their lessons provide options for students to (a) regulate and monitor their own learning, (b) maintain effort and motivation, (c) engage and sustain interest. As lessons and learning activities are developed, teachers reflect on how information is presented to students. Teachers provide options that allow all students to (a) engage in higher levels of comprehension, (b) explore symbols and expressions, and (c) focus on what needs to be learned. Teachers create learning experiences that

Figure 5.5 • *SoLD Principles of Practices*

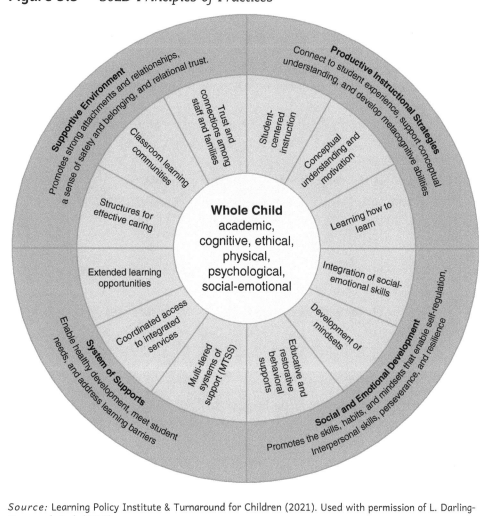

Source: Learning Policy Institute & Turnaround for Children (2021). Used with permission of L. Darling-Hammond et al. (2021).

provide options for all students to (a) act strategically, (b) express themselves, and (c) physically respond to what is being learned (Meyer et al., 2014).

We agree with Janet Nicol (2017) that students with disabilities can learn and thrive when we remove systemic barriers to their learning such as:

> (a) Making classroom materials accessible, (b) providing flexible seating and classroom arrangements that promote and allow students to communicate, (c) provide accommodations without the stigma of identifying deficits, (d) establish routines so that students know what to expect,

> (e) activate background knowledge and schema as a regular part of instruction, (f) establish goals and objectives so that students know why and what they are doing. (Nicol, 2017)

In our work with students with disabilities, we use the following examples of classroom practices that support the UDL format and promote learning for all students which are recommended by Cook and Rao (2018) and Spencer (2011):

- *Post lessons goals*
- *Give students the same task but with different formats*
- *Create a flexible learning environment where students have a choice in working with others or by themselves*
- *Give regular feedback on learning outcomes*
- *Provide opportunities for self-reflection for all students*
- *Scaffold learning before-during-after the lesson*
- *Provide variety in text materials: visual and audio formats, as well as printed text*

Instructional Delivery Systems

Instructional delivery systems can be face-to-face, online synchronous, asynchronous, or hybrid. As educators, our work should be on blending direct and active instruction to help students learn and engage in the content through multiple methods. The instructional delivery system should focus on assisting students to be active, engaged learners. All instruction should be based on goals, processes, expectations, and timelines. As students master content, we want them to engage in the development of their speaking, listening, reading, writing, and critical thinking skills. We support Tucker et al.'s (2017) advantages of blended learning; the advantages of blended learning are that it incorporates the best practices of teaching and learning through its use of personalization, agency, authentic audience, connectivity, and creativity.

Story From the Field #14

During a recent classroom visit, we observed students engaged with electronic devices that served as e-worksheets. Students engaged in rote skill and drill activities without the opportunity to probe questions, summarize, and draw conclusions using their meta-cognitive abilities. We concluded that these students were engaged in electronic page turning without active engagement in learning.

One of the reasons technology could be used in this way is to keep students quiet and busy. Too often we have observed teachers using electronic devices as classroom management tools rather than having students use the device for active and enhanced learning.

Stop and Reflect

1. Are your students using technology in productive ways that also help them build metacognitive abilities while engaging in meaningful learning?

2. How do you prevent using technology as a classroom management tool?

Reflect, Monitor, and Provide Feedback for Learning Recovery and Acceleration

> *Feedback is information about how we are doing in our efforts to reach a goal.*
> —Grant Wiggins (2013)

We believe that student feedback needs to be timely, actionable, and relevant. We agree with Hanna Hart (2021) who maintains that feedback is most effective when it is grounded in a growth mindset and intended to promote learning and understanding. Educators who wish to ensure that the feedback offered to their students is relevant need to incorporate the following key components by Grant Wiggins (2013).

Key components of effective feedback:

1. *Goal-referenced: Students should be able to use the feedback to reach a goal.*
2. *Tangible and transparent: The results should be clear to students and teachers.*
3. *Actionable: Students should know what to do with the feedback.*
4. *User-friendly: Students should be able to understand and know what to do with the feedback. This is especially true for students who can become overwhelmed or confused with too much information.*
5. *Timely: Students should not have to wait too long to get meaningful feedback.*
6. *Ongoing: Students should get several opportunities to improve.*
7. *Consistent: Students should receive feedback that is accurate, believable, and consistent.*

We believe that feedback is ongoing and for it to be equitable, it must move students toward their learning goals. As important as feedback is, we have discovered that many of the teachers we encounter are more comfortable examining summative assessments than they are in addressing formative assessments, in which feedback and practice are daily occurrences for students.

Reflecting on Our Equity Practices

We encourage educators to implement the following to address equity in the classroom: (a) Reframe our own deficit-minded views about our students' academic needs and capabilities to ones grounded in equity; (b) Add content relevant to students' lived experiences, and cultural knowledge; (c) Implement instructional practices that ensure that all of our students are active learners; and (d) Establish a routine of being critically reflective about our own teaching practices. We encourage educators to examine their own equitable practices using the Culturally Responsive Teaching Checklist found in Appendix E. We have found the following self-reflective questions adequate guides for changing our own practices:

Critical Self-Reflection Questions

1. *What went well in this lesson? Why?*
2. *What problems did I experience? Why?*
3. *Was it student-centered? Why? Why not?*
4. *What could I have done differently?*

5. *What did I learn from this experience that will help me in my next lesson?*
6. *What did my students teach me?*
7. *Was I well-prepared and organized?*
8. *What could I have done differently to reach all of my students?* (based upon The Center for Teaching and Learning Excellence: Albertus Magnus College [n.d.])

We contend that educators who incorporate equity for all of their students must be intentional. Ensuring all students will receive instruction that is equitable means recognizing that we remove the stigma attached to many of our students, including those with disabilities. Eliminating deficit language allows us to focus on the whole child. It is essential to activate and build the background knowledge needed for new concepts. This means that instructional scaffolds must be offered throughout the learning event. Finally, including children with disabilities in the general education classroom allows them to learn with their peers. We support providing extra support, tutoring, technology, and learning experiences in the regular classroom rather than constantly disrupting the learning by sending these children out of the classroom for academic support.

We contend that teachers who do not believe that students can learn challenging content will not offer appropriate instruction that promotes equitable classroom practices. As teachers are organizing their classrooms for success, we recommend that the research-based, *Equitable Classroom Practices Observation Checklist* created by the Equity Initiatives Unit of the Montgomery County Maryland Public Schools (2010) be implemented. As teachers plan their classrooms, they can determine if their practices are equitable.

Checklist of Strategies to Use That Promote Engagement, Personal Reflection, and Cultural Relevance

We have found the following equitable practices effective:

- scaffolding;
- reciprocal teaching;
- text talks, close reading;
- teaching students to *learn-how-to-learn* and embrace their metacognitive abilities;
- productive struggle;

- access to rigorous math tasks;
- direct explicit instruction with modeling;
- small group instruction;
- high student engagement connected to cultural relevance.

Take Action

Now that you have explored the importance of utilizing equitable instruction, act on your learning by completing the following application.

Read, Respond, and Reflect

Reread the Stories From the Field and reflect on your own teaching. Answer the questions below.

Let's Reflect

- Does this teaching approach address my student's learning outcomes and objectives?
- Will the instructional approach provide guided and independent practice within a meaningful context?
- Does this instructional approach allow for explaining examples, modeling strategies, classifying concepts, and demonstrating tasks?
- Does this instructional approach engage my students in active learning?
- Will this instruction allow for multiple means of student engagement?

Respond

- Does this instruction provide a variety of responses to indicate student learning?
- Will my students be able to use what is being taught across disciplines?
- Are you currently providing effective instruction that incorporates equitable practice?

SUMMARY

Effective instruction requires thoughtful planning, engages students in active learning, and offers students a variety of ways to demonstrate their learning. Effective instruction allows teachers to use a variety of approaches such as scaffolding, direct instruction, indirect instruction, interactive learning, and experiential learning to meet students' *just-in-time* learning. This is provided during

Tier 1 as a part of the Core Classroom Instruction. Meaningful instruction focuses on helping students develop the metacognitive tools they need as they are learning how to learn. Students engage in the productive struggle when they engage in practices that allow them to problem-solve, explore possible answers, discuss options and confusions, and analyze their own mistakes in a safe and supportive environment. Teachers who engage in equitable practices reflect on how they are supporting and guiding their students' learning; this is especially important for students with disabilities. We believe that equitable practices are the cornerstone for helping students master the core skills in literacy, numeracy, critical thinking, and problem-solving. Throughout this chapter, recommendations have been provided for teachers to provide learning equity and learning excellence.

 TIME TO DIG IN TOOLS

Activity	Description	Research Support and Reference	Link
The Rigor Framework	The Ready for Rigor framework lays out four separate practice areas that are interdependent. When the tools and strategies of each area are blended together, they create the social, emotional, and cognitive conditions that allow students to more actively engage and take ownership of their learning process.	Hammond, Z. L. (2015). *Culturally responsive teaching and the brain*. Corwin.	Ready for Rigor Framework https:// qrs.ly/ v6eqdysf
Academic Success for All Students: A Multi-Tiered Approach	This *Edutopia* video, and several other articles, highlight how a school in Florida is using a multi-tiered system of support framework to meet the needs of every child.	*Edutopia*/Positive Behavioral Interventions & Supports	https:// qrs.ly/ 68eqdzg https:// qrs.ly/ lkeqdzi
Six Scaffolding Strategies to Use With Your Students	This resource describes six scaffolding strategies that educators can use to support student learning: (1) show and tell (2) tap into prior		https:// qrs.ly/ apeqdzm

Activity	Description	Research Support and Reference	Link
	knowledge (3) provide time to talk (4) pre-teach vocabulary.		
100 Days of Professional Learning: "Teaching and Using Mathematics to understand our world."	Videos and resources created by NCTM members to include math activities related to making sense of world events.	National Council of Teachers of Math https://www.nctm.org/online-learning	https://buff.ly/3FQW24L
Khan Academy	Khan Academy is an American non-profit educational organization created in 2008 by Sal Khan. Its goal is to create a set of online tools that help educate students. The organization produces short lessons in the form of videos. Its website also includes supplementary practice exercises and materials for educators.	Murphy, R., Gallagher, L., Krumm, A., Mislevy, J., & Hafter, A. (2014). *Research on the use of Khan Academy in schools.* SRI Education.	https://www.khanacademy.org/
Implement strategies of high expectations, Stretch It, No Opt Out, Without Apology and Right is Right	*Teach Like a Champion* provides educators with a set of techniques, a shared vocabulary, and a framework for practice that equip teachers to achieve dramatic results.	Lemov, D. (2014). *Teach like a champion 2.0.* John Wiley & Sons.	Four Teach Like a Champion Strategies https://teachlikeachampion.org/ https://qrs.ly/sveqdzr

(Continued)

(Continued)

Activity	Description	Research Support and Reference	Link
Intellectual Preparation Protocol	Intellectual Preparation allows teachers to create, revise, and internalize high-quality lessons before delivering them to students to make sure all students can find success with rigorous instruction.	Achievement First Lesson Preparation Protocol	Lesson Level Intellectual Preparation Protocol https://qrs.ly/fheqdzt
Notice and Wonder Protocol	When students become active doers of mathematics, the greatest gains of their mathematical thinking can be realized. The process of sense-making begins when we create classrooms full of curious students' thoughts and ideas. By asking, "What do you notice? What do you wonder?" We help our students see problems in big-picture ways.	National Council of Mathematics Teachers	https://www.nctm.org/noticeand wonder/
Close Reading	Thoughtful, critical analysis of the text that focuses on understanding and meaning.	Reutzel, D. R. (2016). *The habits of close reading*. https://www.curriculumassociates.com/-/media/517 54a18c56743e1b1bf3 d674d94ce02.ashx	https://qrs.ly/3feqe03 Close Reading Annotation Symbols Poster and Bookmarks https://qrs.ly/bceqe06

Activity	Description	Research Support and Reference	Link
Identify priority content for each grade level	Focus on "priority instructional content," as identified by Student Achievement Partners.	Student Achievement Partners	https://qrs.ly/naeqe0f
Engaging in a Text Talk	*A Text Talk* is a protocol for setting educators up to internalize the text before instruction.	The Achievement Network	Text Talk Protocol https://qrs.ly/naeqe0f https://qrs.ly/5perqcd
Text Talk for Student Engagement in Reading	Activities designed to cultivate engaging discussions include book clubs, collaborative reasoning, instructional conversations, and literature circles.	International Reading Association: https://www.literacyworldwide.org/get-resources/ila-e-ssentials/8045	https://qrs.ly/l8eqe0h
Panorama Multi-tiered System of Support RTI	Incorporation of assessment, instruction, and decision-making within a tiered model. This is designed to address multiple systems into one coherent system.	Mcintosh, K., & Goodwin, S. (2016). *Integrated multi-tiered systems of support: Blending RTI and PBIS*. Guilford Publications.	https://qrs.ly/ozeqe0l

(Continued)

(Continued)

Activity	Description	Research Support and Reference	Link
A pathway to equitable math instruction Toolkit	Provides resources and guidance for use in curriculum development and lesson design.	Student Achievement Partners. (2021). *2020–2021 Priority instructional content in ELA/literacy and mathematics.* https://achievethecore.org/page/3267/priority-instructional-content-in-english-language-arts-literacy-and-mathematics	https://equitablemath.org/
Literacy for All: Equitable Practices for Reading and Dyslexia	Resources and videos on how to address reading struggles and best practices for teaching all students to read.	National Center on Improving Literacy. https://improvingliteracy.org/	https://qrs.ly/25eqe0o
NCTM: Math Resources: Teaching Mathematics to Understand Our World	Using Math to Make Sense of Our World: Pandemics, Viruses, and Our Actions.	National Council of Teachers of Mathematics: https://www.nctm.org/Coronavirus-and-Pandemics-Math-Resources/	https://qrs.ly/l6eqe0s
Reciprocal Teaching	Strategy that asks both students and teachers to share the role of the teacher in which predicting, question generating, clarifying, and summarizing are exchanged.	Reading Rockets: a national multimedia project that provides research-based strategies, lessons, and activities.	https://qrs.ly/fmeqe10 See Appendix 6 for Summarize, Clarify, Predict, and Question Cards for Students

Activity	Description	Research Support and Reference	Link
How Learning Happens: *Edutopia*	Strategies are illustrated that enact the science of learning and development in schools and other learning settings. There are several series on various topics, such as fostering positive relationships, cultivating a belonging mindset, foundational skills and academic confidence, and positive conditions for learning.	Video Series https://www.edutopia.org/how-learning-happens	https://www.edutopia.org/how-learning-happens
Differentiating Instruction: Finding Manageable Ways to Meet Individual Needs (ASCD)	Tailoring instruction to meet the individual needs of students. The content, product, process, or environment can be differentiated to meet students' needs.	Tomlinson, C. A. (2000 August). *Differentiation of instruction in the elementary grades. ERIC digest. ERIC Clearinghouse on elementary and early childhood education.* https://files.eric.ed.gov/fulltext/ED443572.pdf	https://qrs.ly/c8eqe17
Preparing to Teach in a Culturally Relevant Way	Article on preparing to teach in a Culturally Relevant way	Amoako-Kayser, A & Keown, K. (2022). Preparing to teach in a culturally relevant way: Part 5 of lessons from the field: Understanding culturally relevant pedagogy in high-quality instructional materials.	https://qrs.ly/soerqr7

(Continued)

(Continued)

Activity	Description	Research Support and Reference	Link
Bridge to Grade Level Math 5-Part System	Chrissy Allison suggests ways to create a Bridge to Grade-Level Math for secondary teachers. Teachers and leaders working with students with significant unfinished learning will benefit from hearing the critical steps to catching students up in mathematics.	Bridge to Grade Level Math A Math System to Address Unfinished Learning	https://qrs.ly/4ferqco

CHAPTER 6

DESSERT

Engagement and Acceleration

> Student engagement is the pathway to student achievement.
> —Pedro Noguera (2021)

Figure 6.1 • *Murray and Turner's (2021) Five-Course Framework for Accelerated Learning*

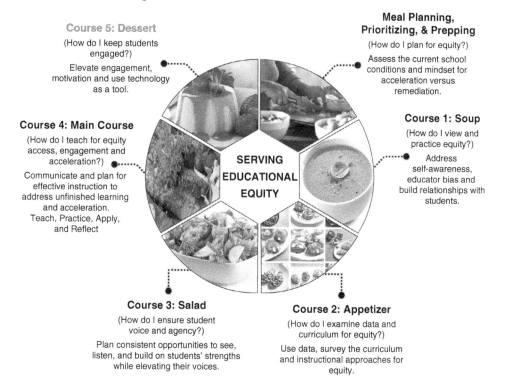

Course 5: Dessert
(How do I keep students engaged?)
Elevate engagement, motivation and use technology as a tool.

Meal Planning, Prioritizing, & Prepping
(How do I plan for equity?)
Assess the current school conditions and mindset for acceleration versus remediation.

Course 4: Main Course
(How do I teach for equity access, engagement and acceleration?)
Communicate and plan for effective instruction to address unfinished learning and acceleration. Teach, Practice, Apply, and Reflect

Course 1: Soup
(How do I view and practice equity?)
Address self-awareness, educator bias and build relationships with students.

SERVING EDUCATIONAL EQUITY

Course 3: Salad
(How do I ensure student voice and agency?)
Plan consistent opportunities to see, listen, and build on students' strengths while elevating their voices.

Course 2: Appetizer
(How do I examine data and curriculum for equity?)
Use data, survey the curriculum and instructional approaches for equity.

ENGAGEMENT AND STUDENT INTERESTS IN LEARNING ACCELERATION

In our Five-Course Framework for Accelerating Learning, we use our dessert course as an analogy for student engagement; see Figure 6.1. This stage of our multistep process is pivotal to student learning. Like the *dessert* course is to the meal, it is the stage that keeps students plugged into the learning experience. Mutually respectful learning environments are created when educators use students' interests and curiosities to accelerate student learning. As schools think about ways to recover student learning, engagement has to be at the forefront of educators' minds. The New Teacher Project (TNTP, 2018), in their groundbreaking article, *The Opportunity Myth*, concluded that deep engagement was a critical factor to improving student learning. Deep engagement occurs when one is acutely focused and emotionally, physically, and mentally engaged in a task (Teach & Kids Learn, 2017).

This chapter supports the SoLD Principles of *Productive Instruction* and *Social and Emotional Development*. We declare that learning is social, emotional, as well as academic. For students to learn, they have to engage in conceptual understanding and motivation. Students' perceptions of their abilities influence their own learning. We embrace equity as an avenue to learning acceleration as we focus on educating the whole child.

One recent Gallup study, including 128 schools and more than 110,000 students, found that student engagement and hope were significantly positively related to student academic achievement progress (growth) in mathematics, reading, and all subjects combined, along with postsecondary readiness in mathematics and writing (Reckmeyer, 2019). Active student engagement supports academic progress.

We have heard the rallying cry for robust engagement and better morale in nearly every school we consult. The recent disruption in teaching and learning focused squarely on the need to increase student motivation. The EdWeek Research Center (Figure 6.2) surveyed students and teachers after the first half of the 2020–2021 school year and found that student motivation and morale were significantly lower than they were before the worldwide pandemic (EdWeek Research Center, 2021).

This is a trend that we want to address with a sense of urgency, as *"student engagement is the pathway to student achievement"* (Noguera, 2020). As schools address unfinished learning and reimagine teaching and learning, motivating students will require teachers to expand their instruction and create highly engaging classrooms. We believe that teachers who want their students to be knowledgeable, resourceful, critical thinkers, and problem-solvers need to

Figure 6.2 • *Student Motivation and Morale*

No Change	Less Motivated	More Motivated

26% · 24% · **50%** · 50%

Half of all students report
less motivation compared
to pre-pandemic.
Among teachers, 87%
viewed student motivation as lower.

No Change	Lower	Higher

23% · 28% · **49%** · 49%

Nearly half of all student
reported lower morale
compared to pre-pandemic.
Among teachers, 82%
viewed student morale as lower.

Source: Adapted from Toth (2021).

reflect on the learning environment they want to create for these students. We embrace the five dimensions of powerful classrooms: (a) content, (b) cognitive demand, (c) equitable access to content, (d) agency, ownership, and identity, and (e) formative assessment. They support teaching robust understanding (TRU) (Schoenfeld, 2016). These dimensions promote understanding that leads to richer content, more student engagement, and more productivity.

Instruction that adjusts to the student's needs and active student participation leads to learning recovery. Instruction that is sensitive to the cultural needs of students supports active engagement. We contend that classrooms in which culturally responsive teaching is addressed serve to engage and motivate students. See Appendix F for a framework for culturally responsive teaching. In our work, we visit schools where students are actively engaged or not actively engaged. We invite you to read the following Stories From the Field to assess the levels of engagement.

Story From the Field #15: Classroom One

As we walked toward the classroom, we could hear students in conversation. They were animated and excited exchanging ideas about the book *Charlie and the Chocolate Factory* by Roald Dahl (1964). One student exclaimed, "This book was better than the first one we read!" Another one shouted, "No, the best part of the book happened when he entered the factory." As the teacher circulated the classroom, students bantered, debated, and engaged in a lively conversation expressing views about the characters, events, and storylines. Students were exchanging ideas as they prepared to write a shared summary of the text using a poster board for a PowerPoint presentation that would be presented later to the entire class. The children reflected on their goals and worked on their summary through think-pair-share activities. The teacher served as an observer and participated by answering specific questions posed by groups of working children.

Story From the Field #16: Classroom Two

We walked into the second classroom, and it was quiet, and the students were compliant. It was a fifth-grade classroom, and students were learning about fractions. The teacher modeled the mathematical thinking and asked students to respond one at a time as their names were called. Students were asked to follow along and write down the steps. The students were working silently with no collaboration or group work except for the occasional students who responded to the teacher's prompts. Students completed the work independently after the teacher's lecture. Students were expected to apply their learning to a series of related mathematic equations they were to solve. The students did not ask questions or exchange ideas.

As you reflect on the two classrooms, ask yourself which class is highly engaging where all are expected to and do participate, or is this a class where select students are actively engaged, and others are passive observers? We support active engagement such as Gallery Walks, Turn-and-Talks, Response Cards, Call and Response, Thumbs up/down, Think-Pair-Share, Human Graph, and In-Class Focus Groups in which all students share their insights.

We have routinely observed quiet and orderly classrooms managed by highly engaged teachers in visiting classrooms. Teachers were animated and diligent in delivering the lesson in these classrooms, often posing questions to one or two students through call and response. After posing the question, one or maybe two students validated to the teacher that all students were "understanding the lesson," but were they? There were careful modeling, quiet classrooms, and nodding students. Teachers questioned students about the posted and often stated learning objectives. By all accounts, the classroom had the recipe for engagement. A few students would respond to the teacher's prompt for answers, yet were *all* actually learning? Could more attention and a more robust understanding of the concept be mastered by posing a single question and allowing all students to actively engage or grapple with a response to the question? Should engagement and cognitive lift be provided to students instead of the teacher? Was there a missed opportunity to answer, or would they offer a call and response? Was there an opportunity to actively engage all students in a dynamic, supportive environment?

When student interests are at the forefront of planning, and a frame of reference is provided, students can connect to what they are learning. Recht and Leslie (1988) connected student retention of skills and background knowledge in their baseball study. In the study, Recht and Leslie examined how prior knowledge affected short-term memory and recall using verbal and nonverbal assessment. Sixty-four junior high students participated, divided into four groups based on two factors: reading ability and prior knowledge of baseball (creating groups of high–high, high–low, low–high, and low–low). Each student was first asked to silently read a narrative text recounting a baseball game's half-inning. Then, the students recreated the narrative by moving wooden pieces around a miniature baseball field and verbally describing what had happened. Next, the researchers asked the participants about their school (to interfere with working memory) before finally asking the students to summarize the half-inning and sort 22 sentences "based on the importance of ideas to the text."

Recht and Leslie (1988) concluded that adequate prior knowledge, strategy instruction, and knowledge base should be equally considered in the design of instruction. Specifically, if educators want to accelerate student learning, it will be essential to consider students' background knowledge in the planning. In all measurements, the students with high prior knowledge performed better, regardless of which reading level they had been grouped.

Stop and Reflect

1. Do you consider the background, skills, and talents of your students when planning for learning acceleration?
2. How do you consider the contributions of your students when planning lessons?

This chapter makes the case that high-quality teaching and learning incorporate students' knowledge and interests and promotes more in-depth student engagement. Engagement is a high-leverage action that has proven to reduce discipline concerns and ensure improved academics (Gregory & Skiba, 2019). When students are engaged and excited about their learning, they are less likely to disconnect from the teaching and learning environment (Figure 6.3).

Figure 6.3 • *Where to Begin*

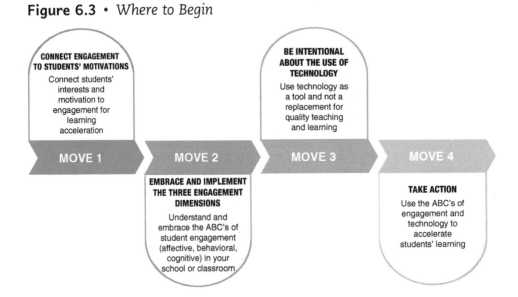

AFFECTIVE, BEHAVIORAL, AND COGNITIVE DIMENSIONS OF ENGAGEMENT

How do you define engagement? Weston Kieschnick (2022) defines engagement as having curiosity, participation, and the desire to persevere. The Universities of North Carolina and Wyoming contend engagement increases student satisfaction, enhances student motivation to learn, and reduces students' feelings of isolation. In our experience serving students for over three decades, one central idea has remained consistent: teachers can enhance student motivation by connecting to students' interests and curiosities. The need for student learning engagement is not a new concept, but the process of making it a reality in classrooms is back in the spotlight (Seif, 2018).

A great way to remember the types of engagement is the ABCs: Affective, Behavioral, and Cognitive. Fredricks et al. (2004) explained student engagement in three main dimensions:

- **Affective Engagement**—Students' feelings, especially toward the subject or course they are studying, their teacher, their peers, their overall academic experience, and regardless of whether they feel the lessons actually have value.

- **Behavioral Engagement**—Students' participation in lessons, such as attendance and concentration levels, as well as their involvement in social aspects of learning, regardless of whether they engage in extracurricular activities.

- **Cognitive Engagement**—Students' motivation and investment in their own education. It also includes the extent to which they take ownership of their own learning, can self-regulate, and wish to pursue personal, and educational goals.

Addressing the ABCs of student engagement and each of the types highlights the limitations of using a short and simple definition for student engagement, as students can simultaneously be engaged in specific ways but disengaged in others. We conclude that full student engagement will require all three dimensions to be met. Achieving this level of engagement will require the appropriate mindset, the use of technology, and vital feedback from educators. Chart 6.1 outlines ways in which educators can address the three engagement dimensions:

Chart 6.1 • *Engagement Dimensions and Action Steps*

Type of Engagement	Action Steps
Affective Engagement	• *Reflect on students' emotional reactions and positive or negative associations in the learning environment* • *Consider the user-friendliness of lessons and encourage teacher-to-student and student-to-student interactions, including appealing activities* • *Reduce student frustration by setting clear expectations*
Behavioral Engagement	• *Identify students' behavioral patterns, social interactions, and general participation during in-person and virtual opportunities* • *Track completeness of activities, such as fully answering the questions in lessons* • *Model and communicate expected learning behaviors before and during assigned tasks*

(Continued)

(Continued)

Type of Engagement	Action Steps
Cognitive Engagement	• *Design and implement tasks using a variety of learning styles to help students access content and display their understanding*
	• *Consider students' curiosity and intellectual interest in course content and academic activities*
	• *Create opportunities to provide feedback and prompt students to share their thoughts and reflections*

Source: Adapted from Hanover Research (2020, p. 4).

Stop and Reflect

Using Chart 6.1, reflect on the affective, behavioral, and cognitive engagement dimensions and the ways you use them in your classroom. Which dimension do you use the most or least? Why?

We are discussing the levels of engagement, which can be defined as being passive, mixed, or highly engaged.

Three Levels of Student Engagement—Passive, Mixed, and Highly Engaged

The levels of engagement refer to the extent of student engagement, and the dimensions (affective, behavioral, and cognitive) refer to the engagement classifications. At the lowest level, students are primarily not engaged in the learning process, and classrooms are almost exclusively teacher-centered. Students are usually passive or compliant. A teacher with passive student engagement usually lectures, asks closed-ended questions that elicit relatively simple responses, generally with only right or wrong answers, or assigns worksheet-type activities requiring relatively simple responses. We assert that students learn best when actively involved in their learning. Today, this "learning by doing" has become known as "experiential learning" or "action learning." Throughout our incorporation of the *SoLD* principles in instruction and learning, we support students' active learning.

Level two of engagement mixes teacher-centeredness with some level of student-centeredness in the teaching and learning process. There are times when the classroom is highly teacher-centered, but also when students are more engaged through structured group activities, class discussions, activities such as the development of timelines or compare or contrast activities, and the like.

At level three, the highest level of engagement, teacher-centeredness is rare. Students are fully and most frequently engaged in the learning process. Teachers act more like coaches and support independent-collaborative learning. Students are actively engaged in the learning process when they use visual organizers, research tasks, coach each other, ask and answer questions, present open-ended discussion questions, complete authentic projects and tasks, participate in simulations, and role plays, and participate in other highly engaging activities. We embrace the highest level of engagement to reclaim lost learning and promote academic advancement in classrooms.

Stop and Reflect

1. Which level of student engagement currently exists in your classroom? How will you ensure that the highest student engagement frequently occurs in your classroom?
2. Are students doing most of the talking in your classroom? If not, how can you increase student talk in your classroom?

Motivation

Motivation increases learning (Theobald, 2006). We contend that student learning is based on their own motivation and the motivational support that teachers provide. Teachers help students develop interest, involvement, and ownership of their learning, which enhances motivation. We offer students choices, engage them in learning how to *learn* through metacognitive strategies, and promote learning in a supportive environment. The National Board for Professional Teaching Standards (Wilcox, 2018) recommend five key strategies for enhancing motivation: (a) Promote growth rather than a fixed mindset so that students see learning complex concepts as a challenge that can be mastered, (b) Develop meaningful and respectful relationships so that our students can feel secure in the classroom, (c) Create a collaborative work environment so that students understand they are a "community of learners," (d) Establish high expectations and clear goals so that students have a purpose and meaning for their work, and (e) Seek to inspire students by providing examples of success stories in which hard work, sacrifice, and proactive behaviors are shared. The **SoLD** principles of creating a strong learning environment, using productive instructional strategies, engaging in the social and emotional development of the whole child, and putting in place strong support systems allow us to focus on the academic and socioemotional well-being of our students.

We encourage teachers to reflect on their motivational practices. We recommend that teachers use short surveys or inventories to determine the motivation and attitudes of students. To explore students' opinions and viewpoints about their motivation, reading, learning, and their school, we have used the *Elementary Reading Attitude Survey* (McKenna & Kear, 1990) and several questions from the *Elementary School Student Survey* (Anderson-Butcher et al., 2013; CAYCI, 2015). We encourage teachers to explore student motivation by using surveys, inventories, and classroom discussions. Teachers can build a positive classroom learning communities by exploring, respecting, and embracing students' opinions about engagement, motivation, and learning (Chart 6.2).

Chart 6.2 · Take Action

Answer each question to indicate how you feel: Yes, Somewhat/Maybe, No

1. I have a positive attitude about my school.
2. I like the challenge of learning new things in school.
3. I am confident in my ability to manage my school work.
4. I work hard at school.
5. I try my best at school.
6. I enjoy coming to school.
7. I have a good relationship with my teacher.
8. I have a good relationship with the other adults at my school.
9. I have a good relationship with my classmates.
10. I am proud to be at my school.
11. I feel like I belong at my school.
12. When I have a problem, I get help from my teacher.
13. I go to my teacher for help when I need it.
14. My teacher wants me to learn a lot.
15. I know that I am smart.

Source: Adapted from the Community and Youth Collaborative Institute (CAYCI) School Experience Survey for Elementary Students (2015).

Stop and Reflect

How do you support the motivation of your students?

We recommend that you examine your students' motivation for learning. Once you have examined your current practices, reflect on how you can enhance the motivation and engagement of your students so that your classroom embraces structure for effective caring and building a classroom learning community.

THE ROLE TECHNOLOGY AND LEARNING ACCELERATION

Story From the Field #17: Classroom One

During an instructional walk, we observed a fourth-grade classroom where a teacher asked students to complete a series of online activities. Students were to visit multiple software programs, complete isolated activities, and complete the activities within a thirty-minute timeframe. She displayed the timer on the screen. No learning outcomes or objectives were provided, and there was limited student–teacher interaction. This event looked like busy work instead of a quality teaching and learning experience. At the end of the timeframe, no discussions were held, no feedback was given, and no assessment was offered of student learning.

Story From the Field #18: Classroom Two

On another instructional walk, we observed a fourth-grade classroom where the students and teacher were discussing learning outcomes, activities, and performance measures. In this classroom, learning objectives and outcomes were posted and stated. There were extensive student–teacher interactions and discussions. Students were deciding which of two software programs could be best used to meet learning objectives. Explicit instructions were given for using the software including how and why this software could enhance their learning. Each student had a notebook for capturing thoughts, questions, and comments to be discussed in the class. Student performances with the online activities were captured and analyzed by the classroom teacher. The teacher facilitated discussion by walking around the room answering questions and providing immediate feedback.

> Technology will never replace great teachers, but technology in the hands of great teachers is transformational.
> —George Couros

We call this chapter the dessert because students love technology just as much as dessert. Technology can quickly enhance learning and motivation, as younger students are easily engaged with special treats such as candy or ice cream. However, we contend that just as dessert can be satisfying and motivating, too much of it can make a person ill. We approach the use of technology the same way. When educators place too much emphasis on technology and allow it to drive teaching and learning, the engagement and objectives of teaching and learning can become lost. We embrace the idea that technology can enhance these learning experiences but should not be a replacement for the quality instruction teachers can provide. We support teachers using computer-based performance feedback to inform instruction. Technology as a "stand-alone" intervention and "bells and whistles" program should not be relied on to increase student engagement for learning recovery and acceleration. Teachers should reflect on how they want their students to use the software to inform their data, instruction, and practice. Evaluating software includes examining it for both efficacy and user-friendliness; see Figure 6.4. Barbara Blackburn in "How Technology Can Increase Rigor in the Classroom" reminds us that "*technology that increases rigor promotes higher order thinking, not rote level tasks*" (Blackburn, n.d., https://www.teachthought.com/pedagogy/rigor-in-the-classroom).

We support integrating technology, pedagogy, and content in advancing learning (Punya & Koehler, 2006). As Ruben Puentedura (2006) points out, incorporating technology into learning should be done in meaningful ways based on purpose, goals, and needs. Teachers who want to use technology in meaningful ways should think about whether the technology acts as a Substitution, Augmentation, Modification, or Redefinition (SAMR) (Puentedura, 2014). While many teachers use Substitution: exchanging in-class lectures and paper worksheets for digital ones and Augmentation: enhancing existing lessons with digital features and multimedia, we support teachers also using Modification: learning management systems to keep track of students' work or Redefinition: in which students engage in activities that take them beyond the classroom such as virtual field trips or creating their blogs and wikis.

Stop and Reflect

1. How do you currently use technology in your classroom?
2. What is my purpose for using this software program?
3. Am I using it for skill and drill?
4. Am I using it to expand the writing capability of my students through word processing?
5. Am I using it for critical thinking and problem-solving?
6. Will it be used to review critical concepts for mastery?

> *Engaging students in the learning environment with technology provides opportunities for a sense of community, accessibility, support, motivation, interest in learning, and self-regulation.*
> —Bond and Bedenlier (2019)

Both teachers and students can benefit from appropriate technology. Technology allows educators to manage their classrooms better, and students are using technology in the application, reinforcement, and extension of their learning. Technology enhances student engagement by (a) increasing emotional and social support, (b) managing classroom operations, (c) supporting students of special populations, (d) addressing different learning styles, (e) supporting differentiation, and (f) providing advanced organizers for new content (Bolden, 2019).

We support using various educational technologies, including videos, applications, online tutorials, games, websites, podcasts, and online programs. In a recent Gallup Poll (2019) on teacher and student use of technology, seven out of 10 students revealed that digital learning tools were fun and helped them learn things independently. In this same poll, educators (65%) indicated that digital learning tools were essential, both in and out of school.

CHOOSING THE RIGHT TECHNOLOGY

We recommend Tony Bates' (2015) Chapter 8: *Choosing and Using Media in Education: The Sections Model* framework for evaluating and choosing the right technology for the school and classroom. The *SECTIONS Model* outlines the criteria for choosing appropriate technology in face-to-face, hybrid, and online learning environments (Chart 6.3).

Chart 6.3 • Bates' (2015) SECTIONS Model: Selecting Technology: Criteria and Questions

Bates' *Sections* Model Framework	Questions for Evaluation
(a) Students	(a) Is the technology accessible and appropriate for all students?
(b) Ease of use	(b) Is the technology simple to use for both teachers and students, and does it include technical and professional support?
(c) Costs & Time	(c) Does the cost justify the time that it takes to set up, implement, manage, and evaluate its effectiveness? Is the technology cost-effective in terms of student learning outcomes?
(d) Teaching Functions	(d) Is the technology designed to enhance regular classroom instruction? Does it use different modalities to reach learning objectives and student learning outcomes?
(e) Interaction	(e) Does the technology offer a balance between student comprehension and student skill development?
(f) Organizational issues	(f) Is institutional/school support easily accessible, helpful, and meets the needs of using the technology? Is networking between students and classes available?
(g) Networking	(g) Is networking between students, teachers, and classes available? Does the technology offer students the benefit of learning from external connections (e.g., museums, historical sites)?
(h) Security & Privacy	(h) Are students provided privacy and security when using the technology? Is students' personal information protected?

Source: Bates (2015).

Figure 6.4 · *Choosing Software Survey*

	Choosing Software: Please rate the tool's efficacy on a scale of 5 = high to 1 = low.				
1. Is the technology tool educator and student friendly?	1	2	3	4	5
2. Does the technology tool provide active student engagement?	1	2	3	4	5
3. Does the technology tool offer inclusivity? Are all students' needs represented?	1	2	3	4	5
4. Does the technology tool promote active student engagement?	1	2	3	4	5
5. Does the technology tool promote students' mastery of skills and understanding of concepts?	1	2	3	4	5

Stop and Reflect

Use the checklist in Figure 6.4 to assess the usability of software to accelerate student learning.

SUMMARY

Just as a dessert captures the essence of a good meal, leaving the diner satisfied and fulfilled, students' learning can be accelerated through their desire, motivation, and curiosity to persevere. We conclude that students learn more when they are behaviorally, emotionally, and cognitively engaged in meaningful learning activities in the classroom. As teachers, we support our students' active engagement by honoring their voices, including *all* students in classroom activities, and allowing them to stretch academically. We support adjusting classroom learning from an emphasis on passive learning to highly engaging activities to ensure learning acceleration. Choosing appropriate software and technology can enhance the teaching and learning experience, and we suggest that teachers choose wisely. Technology serves as a tool for learning, not a replacement for quality instruction and active engagement. Teachers can use appropriate technology to enhance both motivation and active learning.

We have witnessed many classrooms in which teachers prepare thoughtful lessons; however, many of these lessons did not engage students in active learning, enhance their motivation for future learning, or allow students to problem-solve. Engagement and motivation depend on students being given the opportunities to use their metacognitive skills as they learn. We contend that learning recovery and advancement occur when students are actively engaged. As we create learning environments that incorporate students' interests and acknowledge their abilities, we promote equity in the classroom. We conclude that active student engagement leads to student achievement and learning acceleration.

 TIME TO DIG IN TOOLS

Activity	Description	Research Support and Reference	Link
The Opportunity Myth	Students are doing what they are supposed to do and expected to do in high school; however, they are not prepared to succeed after school. They are not ready for college and careers.	TNTP. (2018). The opportunity myth: What students can show us about how school is letting them down—and how to fix it.	https:// qrs.ly/ oxeqe1e
Five Dimensions of Powerful Classrooms	These dimensions include Content, Cognitive Demands, Equitable Access to Content, Agency, Ownership, Identity, and Formative Assessment.	Schoenfeld, A. H., & the Teaching for Robust Understanding Project. . . . The five dimensions of powerful classrooms.	https:// qrs.ly/ 6reqe1k
Jigsaw	Cooperative learning in which students teach concepts to each other.	Aronson, E., Stephen, C., Sikes, J., Blaney, N., & Snapp, M. (1978). *The jigsaw classroom.* SAGE.	https:// qrs.ly/ zkeqe1o
Think-Pair-Share	Collaborative-learning and exchanging ideas used to solve problems.	Gunter, M. A., Estes, T. H., & Schwab, J. H. (1999). *Instruction: A models approach* (3rd ed.). Allyn & Bacon. Tint, S. (2015). Collaborative learning with think-pair-share technique. *An International Journal, 31*(1), 1–11.	https:// qrs.ly/ 1seqe1t

(Continued)

(Continued)

Activity	Description	Research Support and Reference	Link
Wait Time	Increase time is given for students' responses to questions.	Rowe, M. B. (1987). Wait time: slowing down may be a way of speeding up. *American Educator, 11*, 38–43, 47.	https://qrs.ly/d4eqe1w
Elementary Reading Attitude Survey	Survey to determine students' attitudes toward reading. Attitudes can range from very negative to very positive.	McKenna, M. C., & Kear, D. (1990). Measuring attitude toward reading: A new tool for teachers. *The Reading Teacher, 43*, 626–639.	https://qrs.ly/z2eqe25

Technology Resources		
Activity	Description	Link
Kahoot	Kahoot! is a game-based learning platform, used as educational technology in schools and other educational institutions. Its learning games, "kahoots," are user-generated multiple-choice quizzes that can be accessed via a web browser or Kahoot! app.	https://kahoot.com/schools-u/
Padlet	Padlet is a digital tool that can help teachers and students in class and beyond by offering a single place for a notice board.	https://padlet.com/
Mentimeter	Mentimeter is a Swedish company based in Stockholm that develops and maintains an eponymous app used to create presentations with real-time feedback.	https://mentimeter.com
Jamboard	Jamboard makes learning visible and accessible to all collaborators with participants adding virtual sticky notes.	https://jamboard.google.com/u/1/

Technology Resources		
Activity	**Description**	**Link**
Class Tools	Free resources such as fling the teacher, Fakebook, random name picker, and other games can be implemented.	https://classtools.net
EduProtocols	Eduprotocols.com is very useful with links to a ton of resources.	https://Eduprotocol.com
Noisli	Educators can control the background noise in their classrooms with this application to create a perfect sound to work and relax.	https://www.noisli.com/s/db4df50209
Classroom Screen	Teachers can project classroom screens to stimulate engagement in the classroom.	https://app.classroomscreen.com/
Hyperdocs	HyperDocs are digital lesson plans designed by teachers and given to students.	https://hyperdocs.co/find
Teacher Made	TeacherMade takes static PDFs, Word documents, or image files and turns them into digital, interactive worksheets.	https://teachermade.com/
Flippity	Flippity: Google™ Spreadsheet into a set of online flashcards and other cool stuff!	https://flippity.net/
Symbaloo	Symbaloo – Choice board and quick links. Make your own or use premade ones.	http://www.symbaloo.com/home/mix/13eOcRbjEE
Bitly	Bitly addresses allow users to shorten any URL for easy access.	https://bitly.com
Readworks	Free library of e-books, content, curricular supports, and digital tools designed to support literacy and critical thinking.	https://www.readworks.org/

EPILOGUE: A RETURN TO JACOB'S SCHOOL

> Do the best you can until you know better. Then when you know better, do better.
>
> —Maya Angelou

Figure E.1 • *Murray and Turner's (2021) Five–Course Framework for Accelerated Learning*

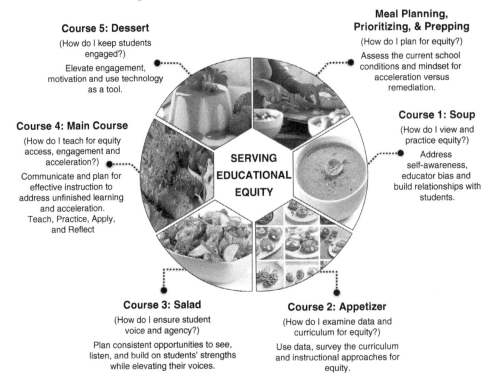

Course 5: Dessert
(How do I keep students engaged?)
Elevate engagement, motivation and use technology as a tool.

Meal Planning, Prioritizing, & Prepping
(How do I plan for equity?)
Assess the current school conditions and mindset for acceleration versus remediation.

Course 4: Main Course
(How do I teach for equity access, engagement and acceleration?)
Communicate and plan for effective instruction to address unfinished learning and acceleration.
Teach, Practice, Apply, and Reflect

SERVING EDUCATIONAL EQUITY

Course 1: Soup
(How do I view and practice equity?)
Address self-awareness, educator bias and build relationships with students.

Course 3: Salad
(How do I ensure student voice and agency?)
Plan consistent opportunities to see, listen, and build on students' strengths while elevating their voices.

Course 2: Appetizer
(How do I examine data and curriculum for equity?)
Use data, survey the curriculum and instructional approaches for equity.

We are working with several school personnel who are implementing our *Five–Course Framework for Accelerated Learning* (see Figure E.1), and as we end our book, we want to share the experiences of one school leader and his staff who are making substantial differences in their school and community. We introduced this school in our first chapter when we described the challenges the staff were facing before they completed their own Strengths, Weaknesses, Opportunities, and Threats (SWOT) analysis. We also discussed how Jacob used the SWOT to identify areas of instructional focus.

Jacob, a principal of an elementary school in the Midwest, reflected on the external national tragedies across his community. Schools had shut down in response to a national health emergency. Many schools were engaging in remote learning for the first time. The repercussions of the murder of George Floyd were being felt throughout the country, and there was a public outcry for his justice. Voting rights were being challenged, and the political divisions across the country were creating havoc in many communities. There were divisions across political party lines, and tensions ran high in his school community. Jacob knew the external situations in our world weighed heavily on the hearts and minds of those within his school community. It was on his mind, and he knew that as the school's leader, he would need to lead the courageous conversations and dialogue that could spark adaptive change in mindset, beliefs, and how teaching and learning would happen at his school. He realized that the very future of the children in his care was at stake. Jacob was reflective about what this time meant, especially in response to the disruptions in teaching and learning. The school would need to reimagine past practices that directly impacted teaching and learning while keeping the important dialogue at the forefront of that approach. Jacob and his staff chose our *Five-Course Framework for Accelerated Learning* as the road map to help the school navigate the difficult conversations that could lead to an equity focus on acceleration and changing practices at every level within the school.

During our frequent conversations, Jacob shared his desire to address the issues weighing heavily on his heart and those of people within his school and community. We discussed the best approach to ensure his teachers, students, and parents were provided a voice. We knew the process would have to allow people to speak about their experiences without judgment. The current teaching and learning practices in the school and the rest of the world need to shift to acknowledge the importance of equity, engagement, and learning acceleration. Adaptive change was underway and our five-course framework could help school educators find a simplistic approach to the complexity of ensuring educational equity that prepares students for college and careers.

Moreover, the 150-year-old educational system that prepared students for the industrial world was being challenged by the need for new practices, such as accelerating student learning and the importance of cognitive engagement, including how we involve parents and use technology. Our (Sonya and Gwen's) message has always been "*We can no longer prepare children for the past; we must help them learn to excel in a technologically advanced society in which they engage in critical thinking and reflective practices.*" This philosophy became more crucial than ever before as the historical ways of grading, schooling, and engaging students were flipped on its head. Students would need to be engaged differently, something we knew from years of experience, but the recent school disruption placed reimagination at the forefront. Students were learning from home, remotely, and learning in new ways. Everyone was impacted in Jacob's community, and a lens for equity and acceleration was the only way forward. The school has begun initiating a changed mindset around its practices regarding remediation, a familiar practice at the school. They are planning collaboratively and allowing data to drive instructional decisions. The school's team is creating a culture of embracing learning at every level.

The focus on educational equity and the best approach to achieve it culminate from our many years of experience working with school leaders. However, it was through this tumultuous time that the opportunity for reimagination and reframing teaching and learning the *Five-Course Framework for Accelerated Learning* was put into practice.

At Jacob's school, we started our process of educational equity using data to confront our perceptions, beliefs, and assumptions, explicitly addressing the brutal fact that our perceptions and thoughts could be tainting how we see our students, each other, and our world. This approach would be the framework and road map to educational equity we suggest in this book. We would navigate the journey of learning more about ourselves, uncovering our mental models, and reexamining our perceived thoughts about the students we serve.

Jacob's school team began a journey of self-discovery and self-reflection that would lead to dignity and cultural empathy for the students, staff, and families. That journey would align the team on a path of collective efficacy toward helping students reach their full academic potential through acceleration. After stamping the road ahead with an *Equity and Inclusion* declaration, his school team would address adaptive change using a SWOT analysis. The road map profoundly influenced Jacob's leadership and the school.

Principal Jacob's Collective School Equity Agreement

We are committed to providing equitable, joyful, real-life educational experiences for our community. We understand the role of race, culture, and socioeconomics in our interactions and work and plan for inclusive interactions within our school. We commit to investing in practices that promote students' success in college and careers for lifelong learning.

After crafting an explicit declaration that could guide the work of teaching and learning at the school, the team engaged in a SWOT analysis to determine the best place to start. The school team ran the SWOT analysis and determined their structures and systems were solid, revealing the need for strengthening data usage to best pinpoint places to accelerate teaching and learning. Teachers and staff reflected on the opportunities available for addressing student misconceptions free of their own biases about students' abilities. The SWOT analysis allowed these educators to assess the present state of teaching and learning without preconceived biases about the students' abilities.

Monthly training with *Equity Matters* and the in-house established school teams led training on implicit bias, and the SWOT offered a great starting point for discussions on what worked and why in the school. The SWOT data independently confirmed strengths, resources, and weaknesses. Members of the school worked as a collaborative team with more cohesion, focus, and purpose as the team prepared for accelerated learning.

Strengths	Weakness
What do you do well to provide educational equity for every child? • We provide wraparound services for students and families. • We offer electronic devices to all students. • We build rapport by learning about students' backgrounds and families. • Our team embraces a growth mindset. • Class Meetings. • Student Data gradually improve, and student work evidence mastery of standards and skills.	*Where can we improve?* • We can improve by getting to know one another better. We can try to work better as a team, and we can have a better understanding of equity. • SEL needs and behaviors of students. • Student buy-in ad voice could be areas of opportunity. • We can improve by having empathy for All. • We can improve by raising the bar on expectations, not just having minimum expects. Allow the students to push themselves in all aspects, not just the educational part. • We can improve how support is given.
Opportunities	**Threats**
What opportunities are available to us? What would we like to achieve? • We can embrace courageous conversations. • User strategies to accelerate student learning. • Create shared agreements.	*What obstacles do we face?* • Schools shutting down and the extended pandemic.

At the time of our book's publication, Jacob's school team continues to reflect and revolve collectively on learning potential, possibilities, and techniques while avoiding the trap of deficit thinking. The group continues to examine their own philosophical beliefs about student capabilities. As a result, they believed they were better prepared to meet their students' academic needs. After gaining an honest appraisal of current conditions, it was time for these educators to look inwardly at motivating factors. These motivating factors drive us and constitute our *why* and the reasons we engage in the vital work of educational equity. This crucial analysis step for planning allowed these teachers to prioritize their actions.

Jacob and his team used the SWOT to determine the best initiatives for acceleration and student engagement to ensure educational equity. As a school leader, he and his school team captured and identified three emerging themes to prepare students for college and careers; those areas were social and cross-cultural empathy and preparation as global citizens. Specifically, the school rallied around understanding one another and their students to increase a sense of belonging at the school. Also, the school staff explored ways to embrace their cultural identities and those of their students in teaching and learning systems and structures. Jacob's school team took the time to reexamine their data, the curriculum, and instructional processes designed to accelerate student learning. Additionally, the school embraced the SoLD principles as they selected instructional strategies, techniques, and technology designed to accelerate the learning of all students. The school reflected on opportunities to garner more parent support to meet acceleration approaches to maximize students' learning.

Recognizing this work is a journey and not an event, Jacob's school continues to reflect and revisit its progress to achieving educational equity for the students they serve. The school has taken on the challenge to embrace the main course this year by focusing on those *SoLD* principles as scientifically based strategies designed to engage and accelerate student learning. Their instructional approaches acknowledge the need for students' cultural backgrounds to be recognized and embraced. They challenge past remediation practices, understanding that those practices can arbitrarily deny students' opportunities and access. The school team works to challenge the status quo, and they stay on the journey to excellence for all students in the curriculum, instruction, and how they use student data. The team plans to engage in those best practices designed to accelerate learning while using technology as a tool to give students a voice and choice in the conversation. The school keeps a learning solutions focus, a reflective spirit, and a positive mindset to collectively engage in all practices designed to prepare their students to reach their full potential. This school recognizes the journey to equity for all students is still underway.

We end with asking educators to embrace the analogy of Linus, the character from the Charlie Brown series, losing his blanket to how educators feel when they first embrace adaptive change efforts to ensure educational equity for the students they serve. There is a feeling of loss when transitioning old practices to newer ones.

We conclude with poet Maya Angelou's quote, "***Do the best you can until you know better. Then when you know better, do better.***" As schools embrace adaptive change to ensure equitable practice that accelerates and engages students, it is okay to reflect on past strategies while forgiving yourself for things you were unaware. It is essential to take a reflective stance on the journey, recognizing that now is the time to think of what to keep and leave behind, permitting yourself to learn, evolve, and grow. It is a journey that has the potential to reap profound benefits for the millions of students who are counting on us to get it right.

APPENDIX A: INSTRUCTIONAL APPROACHES FOR EQUITABLE PRACTICES

Activity (Link)	Description	Research Support and Reference
Use of Students' Names https://qrs.ly/7feqkt5	Acknowledging the student as a person, not a label.	Chambliss, D. F. (2014). Learn your students' names. *Inside Higher Ed*. www.insidehighered. com/views/2014/08/26/ essay-calling-faculty-members-learn-their-students-names
Wait Time https://qrs.ly/d4eqe1w	Increase time given for students' responses to questions.	Rowe, M. B. (1987). Wait time: Slowing down may be a way of speeding up. *American Educator, 11*, 38–43, 47.
Active Instead of Passive Engagement https://qrs.ly/ayer1ww	Talk, write, relate, act out, and apply to new situations.	Cross, P. (1987). Teaching for learning. *AAHE Bulletin, 39*(8), 3–7.
Ask Three, Then Me https://qrs.ly/7oer1xb	Building learning capacity and independence to accomplish challenging tasks by verifying information, collaborating, and communicating.	Teachthought. (2022). *What is 3 before me? A teaching strategy to build capacity in students.* https://www. teachthought.com/ pedagogy/3-before-me/ #:~:text=What%20is% 20'3%20Before% 20Me,reaching%20out% 20to%20the%20teacher

Activity (Link)	Description	Research Support and Reference
Think-Pair-Share https://qrs.ly/pfer1xn	Collaborative learning and exchanging ideas used to solve problems.	Gunter, M. A., Estes, T. H., & Schwab, J. H. (1999). *Instruction: A models approach* (3rd ed.). Allyn & Bacon. Tint, S. (2015). Collaborative learning with think-pair-share technique. *An International Journal, 31*(1), 1–11.
Reciprocal Questioning https://qrs.ly/efer20e	Dialogue where students take on the role of teacher and generate questions.	Oczuks, L. (2003). *Reciprocal teaching at work: Strategies for improving reading comprehension.* International Reading Association.
Reciprocal Teaching https://qrs.ly/5veqku9	Students take the role of teacher while predicting, generating, clarifying, and summarizing.	Palincsar, A. S., & Brown, A. (1984). Reciprocal teaching of comprehension-fostering and comprehension monitoring activities. *Cognition and Instruction, 1*(2), 117–175.
Reciprocal Teaching Cards https://qrs.ly/oder21f https://qrs.ly/tver21k https://qrs.ly/zmer21p	Reciprocal teaching refers to an instructional activity in which students become teachers in small group reading sessions. Teachers model, then help students learn to guide group discussions using four strategies: summarizing, question generating, clarifying, and predicting. Once students have learned the strategies, they take turns assuming the role of the teacher in leading a dialogue about what has been read.	Reading Rockets Reading Rockets. (n.d.). *Reciprocal teaching: Why use reciprocal teaching.* https://www.readingrockets.org/strategies/reciprocal_teaching

(Continued)

(Continued)

Activity (Link)	Description	Research Support and Reference
Close Reading https://qrs.ly/eker21y	Critical analysis of the text that includes identifying key ideas, significant details, and patterns through rereading.	Burke, B. (n.d.). *A look at close reading.* https://nieonline.com/tbtimes/downloads/CCSS_reading.pdf
Anticipation Guide https://qrs.ly/jver23z	Pre-reading guide to scaffold learning by activating background knowledge, providing a purpose/focus for reading, and promoting interest in the topic.	Herber, H. L. (1978). *Teaching reading in content areas.* Prentice Hall.
Concept Maps https://qrs.ly/djer24q	Graphics allow students to relate new knowledge and integrate it into an existing network of concepts. This leads to more meaningful learning and less rote memorization.	Malone, J., & Dekkers, J. The concept map as an aid to instruction in science and mathematics. *School Science and Mathematics, 84*(3), 220–231.
Exit Slips https://qrs.ly/ther24v	Formative feedback that allows students to indicate their understanding in writing.	Marzano, R. (2012). The many uses of exit slips. *Educational Leadership, [online] 70.2:80–81.* http://www.ascd.org/publications/educationalleadership/oct12/vol70/num02/The-Many-Uses-of-Exit-Slips.aspx
Inquiry (I-) Chart https://qrs.ly/r3er24z	Learning log engages students in questioning, reflecting, and summarizing.	Hoffman, J. V. (1992). Critical reading/thinking across the curriculum: Using I-charts to support learning. *Language arts, 69*(2), 121–127.
Gallery Walk https://qrs.ly/wier25i	Students circle while they read, write, and discuss images they see.	Schulten, K. (2011, June 14). The times and the common core standards: Reading strategies for

Activity (Link)	Description	Research Support and Reference
		'Informational Text'. *New York Times.* http://learning.blogs.nytimes.com/2011/06/14/the-times-and-the-common-core-standards-reading-strategies-for -informational-text/
Jigsaw https://qrs.ly/6rerad0	Cooperative learning in which students teach concepts to each other.	Aronson, E., Stephen, C., Sikes, J., Blaney, N., & Snapp, M. (1978). *The jigsaw classroom.* SAGE.
K-W-L https://qrs.ly/h2erad4	Allows students to explore what they know, want to learn, and what they have learned when reading.	Ogle, D. (1986). K-W-L: A teaching model that develops active reading of the expository text. *The Reading Teacher, 39*, 564–570.
Question-Answer Relationships (QAR) https://qrs.ly/5jerad7	Comprehension strategy that establishes the relationship between a type of question being asked and the answer.	Raphael, T. E. (1986). Teaching question-answer relationships, revisited. *The Reading Teacher, 39*(6), 516–522.
Story Maps https://qrs.ly/96eradf	Graphic representation of story elements and their relationships.	Davis, Z. T., & McPherson, M. D. (1989). Story map instruction: A road map for reading comprehension. *The Reading Teacher, 43*(3), 232.
Think-Alouds https://qrs.ly/32eradg	Verbal problem-solving while sharing one's thoughts. "Making invisible mental processes visible."	Silbey, R. (2002). Math think-alouds. *Instructor (1999), 111*(7), 26–27. Wilhelm, J. D. (2001). Think-alouds boost reading comprehension. *Instructor (1999), 111*(4), 26–28.
Visual Imagery https://qrs.ly/8yeradl	Using visualization to clarify meaning.	Hibbing, A. N., & Rankin-Erickson, J. L. (2003). A picture is worth a thousand words: Using visual images to improve

(Continued)

(Continued)

Activity (Link)	Description	Research Support and Reference
		comprehension in middle school struggling readers. *The Reading Teacher*, *569*, 758–762.
List-Group-Label https://qrs.ly/a9erf9k	Categorizing and determining the relationship among concepts.	Nessel, D., & Baltas, J. (2000). *Thinking strategies for student achievement*. National Urban Alliance/Teachers College, Columbia University & Arlington Heights, IL: Skylight Publications.
Semantic Feature Analysis https://qrs.ly/hnerf9w	Focuses on both the vocabulary and concepts needed for comprehension.	Anders, P. L., & Bos, C. S. (1986). Semantic feature analysis: An interactive strategy for vocabulary development and text comprehension. *Journal of Reading*, *29*(7), 610–616.
Word Maps https://qrs.ly/rderfa0	Understanding both the function of concepts in relationships to their attributes.	Rupley, W. H., Logan, J. W., & Nichols, W. D. (1998). Vocabulary instruction in a balanced reading program. *The Reading Teacher*, *52*(4), 336–346.
I Wonder https://qrs.ly/deerfa5	Uses students' own interests and curiosities to help them feel ownership of their learning.	Rumack, A. M., & Huinker, D. (2019). Capturing mathematical curiosity with notice and wonder. *Mathematics Teaching in the Middle School MTMS*, *24*(7), 394–399. https://pubs.nctm.org/view/journals/mtms/24/7/article-p394.xml

Activity (Link)	Description	Research Support and Reference
Notice and Wonder Protocols https://qrs.ly/2berfa7	Students observe a new concept and discuss or write what they see and what they wonder.	Kennefick, K. (2020). Notice and wonder. *Better Lesson.* https://betterlesson.com/strategy/219/notice-and-wonder?from=strategy_details
Math Anchor Charts https://qrs.ly/eyerfao	Process and strategy displays that support students' problem-solving, thinking, and reasoning.	Aly. (2019, September 17) *10 best math anchor charts for elementary school classrooms.* Life with Ones—Instructing Elementary Students. https://www.lifewithonesies.com/best-math-anchor-charts/
RAFT https://qrs.ly/foerfau	Writing strategy that helps students communicate better and understand the role their role as writers.	Santa, C. M. (1988). *Content reading including study systems.* Kendall/Hunt.
Vocabulary Games https://qrs.ly/hyerfb6	Multiple exposures to words in multiple contexts.	Blachowicz, C. L. Z., & Fisher, P. (2000). Vocabulary instruction. In M. L. Kamil, P. B. Mosenthal, P. D. Pearson, & R. Barr (Eds.), *Handbook of reading research* (Vol. 3, pp. 503–523). Erlbaum. Townsend, D. (2009). Building academic vocabulary in after school settings: Games for growth with middle school English language learners. *Journal of Adolescent & Adult Literacy, 53*(3), 242–251.
Paired/Peer Reading https://qrs.ly/mxerfba	Oral reading practice to develop fluency; it supports peer-assisted learning.	Koskinen, P., & Blum, I. (1986). Paired repeated reading: A classroom strategy for developing fluent reading. *The Reading Teacher, 40*(1), 70–75.

(Continued)

(Continued)

Activity (Link)	Description	Research Support and Reference
Choral Reading https://qrs.ly/q1erfbw	Reading in unison to develop fluency, improve sight vocabulary, and enhance reading motivation.	Paige, D. D. (2011). 16 minutes of "eyes-on-text" can make a difference: whole-class choral reading as an adolescent fluency strategy. *Reading Horizons, 51*(1), 1–20.
Reader's Theater https://qrs.ly/f4erfc4	An integrated approach in which students read, listen, and speak Students develop oral reading fluency by reading parts in scripts.	Young, C., & Rasinski, T. (2009). Implementing reader's theater as an approach to classroom fluency instruction. *The Reading Teacher, 63*(1), 4–13.
No OPT OUT: 4 ways to support students who are unwilling or unable to provide answers. The OPT OUT offers assistance from the teacher and classmates. https://qrs.ly/prerfca	The four ways to help students: A. Teacher provides the answer; the student repeats it. B. Another student provides the answer, the original student repeats it. C. Teacher provides a cue; student uses it to get the answer. D. Another student provides the cue and original student uses it to get answer.	Lemov, D. (2021). *Teach like a champion 3.0: 63 Techniques that put on the path to college.* Jossey-Bass.
Equitable Classroom Practices Observation Checklist https://qrs.ly/t7erfch	Montgomery County Public Schools (MCPS) (2010). *Equitable Classroom Practices Observation Checklist: A resource for equitable classroom practices.*	Graves, M. (2010). *Equity initiatives unit – Equitable classroom practices.* Montgomery County Public Schools. https://www.montgomery schoolsmd.org/ departments/ development/resources/ ecp/

APPENDIX B: MATHEMATICS LESSON PLAN

Name of Lesson Grade Level Length of Lesson	Name of Lesson Grade Level Length of Lesson
Lesson One:	**Lesson Two:**
Intellectual Preparation The teacher assigns math problems to students and prepares tips and tricks strategies or mnemonics as they model the steps to solve different math equations.	Intellectual Preparation The teacher finds rich math situations for students to engage with and solves those problems in multiple ways to identify knowledge and skills students might bring to the table and the solutions or strategies they might choose to use.
Objectives • I can understand the meanings and uses of fractions, including the fraction of a set • I can understand that the size of a fractional part is relative to the size of the whole • I can compare fractions using models and number lines. • I can identify equivalent fractions using models, multiplication, division, and number lines. • I can add and subtract like fractions.	Objectives • I can represent adding and subtracting fractions in multiple ways. • I can represent a unit fraction and use the value of the numerator and denominator to compare and order fractions based on their values. • I can use the values of the numerator and denominator to identify equivalent fractions using multiple strategies.
Before The teacher has students complete a quick "warm-up" activity before the actual mathematics lesson. Warm-up activities are computational and similar to what students will practice in class.	Before The teacher displays four warm-up problems on the whiteboard, asks students to take two minutes of quiet independent "think time," and then asks students to share their "noticings and wonderings" with the whole class as the teacher writes them on a shared

(Continued)

(Continued)

Lesson One:	Lesson Two:
	workspace, like an anchor chart. The teacher then highlights the trends from student responses and explicitly prompts students to focus on how they could solve the problem.
During	**During**
The teacher gives students feedback on their Do Now. The teacher calls on one or two students to model their responses to aid students' understanding. The teacher asks students to follow along as they solve the problem for student mastery.	Students begin working independently for a couple of minutes and work with a partner to identify possible solution strategies as a whole class with teacher prompting. After this discussion, students continue to work independently to apply solution strategies. At the same time, the teacher monitors what strategies students are using so the teacher can prompt students to address misconceptions before completing the independent "Cool Down" activity.
After	**After**
The teacher asks students to implement what they learned from the Warm-Up practice activities to prepare them to answer the chapter questions. The teacher monitors the classroom and supports and listens to students as they answer the problems. Students independently complete the "Cool Down" mathematics activities.	The teacher facilitates a class discussion about the solution strategies and new content knowledge to help students consolidate their new understandings ensuring they have mastered the content from anecdotal notes, a class-created anchor chart, or a clear exit ticket.
Acceleration/Remediation Implication	**Acceleration/Remediation Implication**
Plan A – The teacher spends an extra day teaching below-grade-level content, such as the meaning of fractions, to address gaps students may have before this lesson.	Plan B – The teacher begins teaching the lesson, reinforcing critical concepts from earlier experiences in the learning progression within the context of the grade-level content.

APPENDIX C: ENGLISH LANGUAGE ARTS LESSON PLAN

Name of Lesson Grade Level Length of Lesson	Name of Lesson Grade Level Length of Lesson
Lesson One:	**Lesson Two:**
Intellectual Preparation	Intellectual Preparation
• Prepare for the lesson by reviewing and skimming the illustrations, title, and subheadings to set the stage for the reading. • Think about the story elements (characters, setting, plot, and conflict). • Identify vocabulary words that could be challenging to students. • Connect to identified learning objectives and standards. • Develop comprehension questions to check for understanding. • Consider lowering the reading level by changing vocabulary, omitting sections of the text, and reducing the size of the text.	• Analyze text complexity: Lexile, syntax (sentence complexity), vocabulary, use of figurative language, subject maturity, organizational structure, presumed readers' background knowledge, etc. • Compare analysis to current students' readiness to determine scaffolds and supports needed to engage students meaningfully with complex text. • Connect to identified learning objectives and standards. • Develop questions to assist students in meeting the objectives while advancing students' identity development through a culturally relevant approach that builds their skills and understanding of the text.
Objectives	Objectives
• I can understand story elements to comprehend text. • I can define new vocabulary words.	• I can read and comprehend grade-level complex text through a close read using reciprocal teaching strategies (summarizing,

(Continued)

(Continued)

Lesson One:	Lesson Two:
• I can make connections to the text using a "text to self" approach. • I can apply knowledge and understanding of the text through a written response.	clarifying, predicting, and questioning). • I can connect to the text by considering my identity and personal experiences. • I can ask questions to clarify unknown words and sentences.
Before: Prereading • Students preview the text by looking at the cover and title, skim the pages to consider text features and text layout, and read the back cover. • Students make predictions about the text. • The teacher explains new vocabulary.	**Before: Prereading** • Determine the purpose of the text and build background by engaging in a "text talk" with students. • Provide needed background information and scaffolds based on analysis in "intellectual preparation." • Ask students to pose prereading inquiries: "From the title and my quick overview. *I predict the selection will be about...*"; "*What will I learn from this passage?*"; "*Questions I already have about this text are....*" • Review protocols and procedures of what good readers do when they have questions or need clarification.
During • Students read the text alone, with partners, or with teachers depending on grade level. • Students make connections to the text and answer teacher directed comprehension questions.	**During** • Engage students in close reading strategies for active engagement. • Note: Close reading is a process of careful analytical reading. It involves repeated readings, text-based discussion, and (often) written analysis of a complex text.

Lesson One:	Lesson Two:
	• Encourage students to engage in the reading of the text using strategies such as Questioning, Monitoring, Student Text Talks, Teacher Modeling: Echo Reading with Scaffolding, and Reciprocal Teaching Strategies. • Assist students in connecting to their identity and personal experiences through modeling, prompting, and questioning.
After Reading (Summarization and Reflection) • Students complete a written response to the text based on comprehension questions stemming from the learning objectives.	**After Reading** (Summarization and Reflection) • Reflect on the key points: "What did I learn from the text? What was the author's main purpose? How does this connect to my prediction?" • Reflect on text complexity: "Why did the author use {insert style element}?" (Examples: various writing styles such figurative language, text structure, syntax, vocabulary, etc.). • Discussion: "How did this information connect to what I already know? How does it deepen my understanding? What curiosities does it spark?" • Connect learning back to intended standards and lesson objectives through discourse and questioning. Choice Activity: 1. Exit Slip: Here are three points learned about the content, the writing style, about myself, or about the reading/writing connection. 2. RAFT: Write and illustrate (Determine the Role, Audience, Format, and Topic).

(Continued)

(Continued)

Lesson One:	Lesson Two:
Acceleration/Remediation Implication	Acceleration/Remediation Implication
Plan A—The teacher connects the text with standards and objectives. The focus is on comprehension of the text If needed, the teacher provides students with below-level reading materials.	Plan B—The teacher spends more time in the "intellectual preparation" part of planning in order to analyze the text with students as the core focus. The teacher scaffolds the grade-level text using close reading and reciprocal teaching strategies to support students in comprehending the text. Connections are made to text-based evidence and students' identities.

APPENDIX D: READY FOR RIGOR: A FRAMEWORK FOR CULTURALLY RESPONSIVE TEACHING

READY FOR RIGOR: A FRAMEWORK FOR CULTURALLY RESPONSIVE TEACHING

AWARENESS

- Know and own your cultural lens.
- Understand the three levels of culture.
- Recognize cultural archetypes of individualism and collectivism.
- Understand how the brain learns.
- Acknowledge the sociopolitical context around race and language.
- Recognize your brain's triggers around race and culture.
- Broaden your interpretation of culturally and linguistically diverse students' learning behaviors.

LEARNING PARTNERSHIPS

- Reimagine the student and teacher relationship as a partnership.
- Take responsibility to reduce students' social-emotional stress from stereotype threat and microaggressions.
- Balance giving students both care and push.
- Help students cultivate a positive mindset and sense of self-efficacy.
  - Support each student to take greater ownership for their learning.
    - Give students language to talk about their learning moves.

Affirmation · *Instructional conversation* · *Wise feedback* · *Validation*

STUDENTS ARE READY FOR RIGOR AND INDEPENDENT LEARNING

INFORMATION PROCESSING

- Provide appropriate challenge in order to stimulate brain growth to increase intellective capacity.
- Help students process new content using methods from oral traditions.
- Connect new content to culturally relevant examples and metaphors from students' community and everyday lives.
- Provide students authentic opportunities to process content.
- Teach students cognitive routines using the brain's natural learning systems.
- Use formative assessments and feedback to increase intellective capacity.

COMMUNITY OF LEARNERS & LEARNING ENVIRONMENT

- Create an environment that is intellectually and socially safe for learning.
  - Make space for student voice and agency.
- Build classroom culture and learning around communal (sociocultural) talk and task structures.
- Use classroom rituals and routines to support a culture of learning.
- Use principles of restorative justice to manage conflicts and redirect negative behavior.

Source: Hammond, Z. (2013). *The ready for Rigor framework.* Retrieved from https://crtandthebrain.com/wp-content/uploads/READY-FOR-RIGOR_Final.pdf (Used with permission of Corwin)

APPENDIX E: CULTURALLY RESPONSIVE TEACHING CHECKLIST

1. Collaborative Learning Environment:	Consistent	Inconsistent	Not Present	Notes:
a. Creates a learning environment that promotes creativity and unique expression for all students				
b. Arranges the classroom to accommodate discussion *Arranges seating to facilitate student-student discussion; Seating to facilitate teacher-student discussion*				
c. Uses cooperative learning structures *Structures opportunities for students to learn with their peers (Think-Pair-Share, Teammates consult, Jigsaw, Pairs Check, etc.)*				
d. Uses Wait Time *Pauses at least 3-5 seconds to consider the student's response before affirming, correcting, or probing; Pauses following a student's response allowing other students to react, respond, and/or extend*				

1. Collaborative Learning Environment:	Consistent	Inconsistent	Not Present	Notes:
e. Structures heterogeneous and cooperative groups for learning *Uses random grouping methods to form small groups; Explicitly approaches collaborative learning skills to students; Provides opportunities for cooperative groups to process how well they accomplished a task*				
2. Neutralizing Power Dynamics:	Consistent	Inconsistent	Not Present	Notes:
a. Collaborates with students in the education-related development process (e.g., of educational activities, lessons, the learning environment) *Asks students what they want to learn/make, includes their suggestions in lessons*				
3. Inclusive Teaching Techniques:	Consistent	Inconsistent	Not Present	Notes:
a. Incorporates diverse learning styles (visual, auditory, etc.)				
b. Uses a variety of visual aids and props to support student learning *Uses multiethnic photos, pictures, and props to illustrate concepts and content; uses appropriate technology to illustrate concepts and content*				

(Continued)

(Continued)

4. Integrating Students' Lives/Culture:	Consistent	Inconsistent	Not Present	Notes:
a. Uses students' real-life experiences to connect school learning/educational activities to students' lives. *Actively engages students to learn about their lives, interests, and values. Uses examples that are reflective of students' lives to support learning. Encourages students to discuss and reflect upon how activities relate to their experiences*				
b. Incorporates the students' culture into instructional materials *Takes an active role in learning about the students' cultures and considers how materials may be used to support cultural values. Materials are inclusive and culturally unbiased. Uses appropriate multiethnic pictures and props to illustrate concepts and content*				
c. Incorporates cultural examples in teaching and learning. *Adapts curriculum, communication, and approach based upon knowledge of students' cultures and experiences. Examples, demonstrations, prompts and activities*				

4. Integrating Students' Lives/Culture:	Consistent	Inconsistent	Not Present	Notes:
are inclusive and culturally unbiased, meaningful, and understood by all participants. Reflects on implications of how own cultural lens affects teaching				
d. Encourages the unique expression of all students				
Asks questions and allows for and encourages varied and unique responses; provides a variety of tools and opportunities for students to express themselves				
e. Recognizes the uniqueness of all students				
Acknowledges the aspects of their identity that are important to them through the use of examples and questions; highlights and praises unique expression and creativity of individual students				

5. Connects to Resources:	Consistent	Inconsistent	Not Present	Notes:
a. Provides ongoing individualized support to struggling students that incorporates their strengths				
Uses student skills/ talents/insight to help overcome struggles; holistic help, including academic, social, emotional, etc.				

(Continued)

(Continued)

5. Connects to Resources:	Consistent	Inconsistent	Not Present	Notes:
b. Includes the use of community resources (such as libraries, cultural and community centers)				

6. Responds to Context:	Consistent	Inconsistent	Not Present	Notes:
a. Learns about the sociopolitical and community context of the students				
b. Encourages students to develop projects (e.g., essays, presentations) that can address or responds to their or their community's contextual interests or needs. *Guides students in learning about and critically reflecting on their sociopolitical and/or community context; asks questions about what products could address or express their observations*				

7. Professional Development:	Consistent	Inconsistent	Not Present	Notes:
a. Professional development helps staff understand culture				
b. Professional development helps staff reflect on their own cultural backgrounds, experiences, and expectations.				
c. Professional development enhances teacher skill in				

7. Professional Development:	Consistent	Inconsistent	Not Present	Notes:
integrating culturally relevant materials into the content areas				
d. Professional development activities are culturally relevant to the lives of the students				
e. Professional development activities incorporate diverse learning styles				

Source: Used with permission from BECOME 2017; for additional information please contact Dr. Dominica McBride: www.becomecenter.org.

Culturally Responsive Teaching Checklist. BECOME 2017. www.becomecenter.org.

http://www.fcsem.org/uploads/1/4/6/4/14649140/culturally_responsive_checklist_teachers.pdf.

APPENDIX F: 3 BEFORE ME

Source: Artypants. Used with permission.

REFERENCES .

Introduction

Blackburn, B. (2020, September 16). *Four myths about rigor in the classroom*. MiddleWeb. https://www.middleweb.com/34738/four-myths-about-rigor-in-the-classroom/

Blackburn, B. (2008). *Rigor is not a four-letter word*. Eye On Education.

Covey, S. (1990). *The 7 habits of highly effective people*. A Fireside Book: Simon & Schuster.

Darling-Hammond, L., & Edgerton, A. (2021, April 5). Accelerating learning as we build back better. Learning in the time of COVID-19 series. *Learning Policy Institute*. https://learningpolicyinstitute.org/blog/covid-accelerated-learning-build-back-better

Darling-Hammond, L., Flook, L., Cook-Harvey, C., Barron, B., & Osher, D. (2020). Implications for the educational practice of the science of learning and development. *Applied Developmental Science*, *24*(2), 97–140. https://doi.org/10.1080/10888691.2018.1537791

Ferguson, R. F. (2003). Teachers' perceptions and expectations and the black-white test score gap. *Urban Education*, *38*(4), 460–507. http://unamusementpark.com/wp-content/uploads/2015/02/teacher-perceptions.pdf

Learning Policy Institute. (2021). *Equitable & empowering learning for each and every child*. https://learningpolicyinstitute.org/

Learning Policy Institute. (2022). *Whole child education*. https://learningpolicyinstitute.org/issue/whole-child-education

Levin, H. (1987). New schools for the disadvantaged. *Teacher Education Quarterly*, *14*(4), 60–83.

Murray, S. (2021). *Equity matters consulting*. www.equitymattersconsulting.org

National Equity Project. (2020). *Leading for equity framework*. https://www.nationalequityproject.org/resources/frameworks

National Equity Project. (2022). *Education equity definition*. https://www.nationalequityproject.org/education-equity-definition

Peppers Rollins, S. (2014). *Learning in the fast lane: 8 ways to put all students on the road to academic success*. ASCD.

Sinek, S. (2009). *Start with why: How great leaders inspire to take action*. Penguin Group.

TNTP. (2018). *The opportunity myth: What students can show us about how school is letting them down—And how to fix it*. https://tntp.org/assets/documents/TNTP_The-Opportunity-Myth_Web.pdf

Chapter 1

Blackburn, B. (2008). *Rigor is not a four-letter word*. Eye On Education.

Blackburn, B. (2014). *Rigor in your classroom: A toolkit for teachers*. Routledge.

Czupryk, B. (2020, April 30). *Remediation won't fix learning loss, but here is what will.* https://tntp.org/blog/post/remediation-wont-help-students-catch-up-heres-what-will

Delpit, L. (1995). *Other people's children: Cultural conflict in the classroom.* The New Press.

Delpit, L. D. (2012). *Multiplication is for white people: Raising expectations of other people's children.* The New Press.

Dixon, J. (2020, November 17). *Just-in-time vs. Just-in-case scaffolding: How to foster productive perseverance.* Houghton Mifflin.

DiMenna, M. (2021, June 1). *4 lessons from the aftermath of Hurricane Katrina to support pandemic recovery.* https://eab.com/insights/expert-insight/strategy/lessons-aftermath-hurricane-katrina-support-pandemic-recovery/

Ferguson, R. F. (2003). Teachers' perceptions and expectations and the black-white test score gap. *Urban Education, 38*(4), 460–507.

Gonser, S. (2020, April 8). *What past education emergencies tell us about our future.* https://www.edutopia.org/article/what-past-education-emergencies-tell-us-about-our-future

Ladson-Billings, G. (2021). I'm here for the hard reset: Post pandemic pedagogy to preserve our culture. *Equity, & Excellence in Education, 54*(1), 68–78. https://doi.org/10.1080/10665684.2020.1863883

Learned, E. P., Christensen, C. R., & Andrews, K. R. (1969). *Business policy: Text and cases.* RD Irwin, Homewood.

Learning Policy Institute & Turnaround for Children. (2021). *Design principles for schools: Putting the science of learning and development into action.* https://learningpolicyinstitute.org/sites/default/files/product-files/SoLD_Design_Principles_REPORT.pdf

Madsen, D. (2016). SWOT analysis: A management fashion perspective. *International Journal of Business Research, 16*(1), 39–56. https://doi.org/10.18374/IJBR-16-1.3

Murray, S., & Turner, G. (2021). *A five-course framework for accelerated learning.* www.equitymattersconsulting.org

National Equity Project. (2022). *Education equity definition.* https://www.nationalequityproject.org/education-equity-definition

National Council of Teachers of Mathematics. (2018). *Catalyzing change in high school mathematics.* NCTM. www.nctm.org

NCTM. (2021, July). *Continuing the journey. Mathematics learning 2021 and beyond.* https://www.nctm.org/uploadedFiles/Research_and_Advocacy/collections/Continuing_the_Journey/NCTM_NCSM_Continuing_the_Journey_Report-Fnl2.pdf

Paul, H. (2020). *What post-katrina New Orleans can teach schools about addressing COVID learning losses.* Center on Reinventing Public Education. https://www.crpe.org/thelens/what-post-katrina-neworleans-can-teach-schools-about-addressing-covid-learning-losses

Pearson, A. (2019, May 23). *Loving our kids to failure—How generous grading can hurt students.* Emerging EdTech. https://www.emergingedtech.com/2019/05/loving-our-kids-to-failure-how-generous-grading-can-hurt-students/

Pepper-Rollins, S. (2014). Learning in the fast last. *Ways to put ALL students on the road to academic success* (*Vol. 8*, pp. 3–6). ASCD.

Piercy, N., & Giles, W. (1989). Making SWOT analysis work. *Marketing Intelligence & Planning*, *7*(5/6), 5–7.

Salciccioli, M. (2021, April). *Understanding and addressing disruptions during COVID-19 pandemic.* CSBA Research and Policy Brief. https://www.csba.org/-/media/CSBA/Files/GovernanceResources/GovernanceBriefs/G-Brief-Learning-Disruptions-May2021.ashx?la=en&rev=1cfbcc998a234fda87f93e2d2ea772d2

Steiner, D., & Weisberg, D. (2020). When students go back to school, too many will start the year behind. *Here's How to Catch Them Up—in Real-Time.* https://www.the74million.org/article/steiner-weisberg-when-students-go-back-to-school-too-many-will-start-the-year-behind-heres-how-to-catch-them-up-in-real-time/

Takabori, A. (2021, June 7). Learning acceleration, not remediation, for a fantastic school year. *Carnegie Learning.* https://www.carnegielearning.com/blog/learning-acceleration-not-remediation/

Thomas Fordham Institute. (2021, March 23). *The acceleration imperative: A plan to address elementary students unfinished learning in the wake of covid 19.* https://files.eric.ed.gov/fulltext/ED613178.pdf

TNTP. (2021, May 23). Accelerate, don't remediate: New evidence from elementary math classrooms. https://tntp.org/publications/view/accelerate-dont-remediate

TNTP. (2020, December). *Learning acceleration: Planning for acceleration: 2021 and beyond* [Powerpoint]. New Mexico Public Education Department. https://webnew.ped.state.nm.us/wp-content/uploads/2020/12/Learning-Acceleration-Guide-Introduction-Acceleration-Planning-Introduction.pdf

TNTP. (2018). *The opportunity myth: What students can show us about how school is letting them down—And how to fix it.* https://opportunitymyth.tntp.org/

UnboundEd Learning, Inc. (2020). *The intersection of equity and math instruction. Licensed under CC-BY-NC-ND* [PowerPoint slides]. https://lessons.unbounded.org/downloads/30076/preview

UNESCO. (2020). *Don't remediate, accelerate! Effective catch-up learning strategies: Evidence from the United States.* Global Education Coalition. ED/GED/2020/01.

Weems, C. F., Taylor, L. K., Cannon, M. F., Marino, R. C., Romano, D. M., Scott, B. G., & Triplett, V. (2010). Post traumatic stress, context, and the lingering effects of the Hurricane Katrina disaster among ethnic minority youth. *Journal of Abnormal Child Psychology*, *38*, 49–56.

Weisberg, D., Webb, R., & Steiner, D. (2020). *Don't remediate – Accelerate.* Presentation for the National Charter Schools (NCSC). Virtual Sessions. https://gateway.on24.com/wcc/eh/2395807/lp/2518785/don%27tremediate--accelerate%21

ZEARN. (2021, June 23). Accelerate, don't remediate: New research study from TNTP and ZEARN. [Video]. YouTube. https://www.youtube.com/watch?v=nNjvYvW38EI

Chapter 2

Alexander, M. (2016, April 13). *The warm demander: An equity approach.* https://www.edutopia.org/blog/warm-demander-equity-approach-matt-alexander#:~:text=Warm%20demanders%20are%20teachers%20who,the%20warm%20demander%20is%20the

Blease, D. (1983). Teacher expectations and the self-fulfilling prophecy. *Educational Studies*, *9*(2), 123–129.

Bornstein, D. (2015, July 24). Teaching social skills to improve grades and lives. *The New York Times*. https://opinionator.blogs.nytimes.com

Brophy, J. E. (1983). Research on the self-fulfilling prophecy and teacher expectations. *Journal of Educational Psychology*, *75*(5), 631–661.

Cantor, P. (2021, February 23). The future of education: A panel discussion featuring Dr. Pamela Cantor [Video]. *Newsela*. https://go.newsela.com/Bright-Spots-ODC.html

Cantor, P., Osher, D., Berg, J., Steyer, L., & Rose, T. (2018). Malleability, plasticity, and individuality: How children learn and develop in context. *Applied Developmental Science*, *23*(4), 307–337. https://doi.org/10.1080/1088691.2017.1398649

Cole, S. F., Eisner, A., Gregory, M., & Ristuccia, J. (2013). *Helping traumatized children learn: Creating and advocating for trauma-sensitive schools.* Massachusetts Advocates for Children, Trauma and Learning Policy Initiative.

Collins, J. (2001). *Good to great.* Random House Business Books.

Collins, J. (2003). *Good to great.* Random House Business Books.

Comer, J. (1996). *Child by child. The Comer process for change in education.* Better World Books.

Cobb, F., & Krownapple, J. (2020). *Belonging through a culture of dignity. The keys to successful equity implementation.* Mimi and Todd Press.

Delpit, L. D. (2012). *Multiplication is for White people: Raising expectations of other people's children.* The New Press.

Equity Literacy Institute. (2021). *Equity literacy and definitions.* https://www.equityliteracy.org/equity-literacy-definition

Ferguson, R. (2003). *Teacher's perceptions and expectations in the Black-White test score GAP.* https://www.researchgate.net/profile/Ronald-Ferguson/publication/234731262_Teachers%27_Perceptions_and_Expectations_and_the_Black-White_Test_Score_Gap/links/5fc1de55299bf104cf87939a/Teachers-Perceptions-and-Expectations-and-the-Black-White-Test-Score-Gap.pdf

Gorski, P. (2013). *Reaching and teaching students in poverty: Strategies for erasing the opportunity gap.* Teachers College Press.

Gorski, P. (2019). Avoiding equity detours. *Education Leadership*, *76*(7), 56–71.

Gray, L. (2016, October 26). *Educational trauma: The wounds and pains of school.* https://www.huffpost.com/entry/educational-trauma-the-wounds-and-pains-of-school_b_5811121be4b09b190529bfea

Hammond, Z. (2015). *Culturally responsive teaching & the brain.* Corwin.

Harrington, T. (2018, April 6). Educators ask teachers to examine unconscious racial bias. *Ed Source.* https://edsource.org/2018/closing-the-achievement-gap-requires-teachers-to-examine-their-unconscious-racial-bias-teacher-trainer-says/595408

Hannigan, J. D., & Hannigan, J. E. (2016). *Don't suspend me: An alternative toolkit.* Corwin.

Kendi, I. (2019). *How to be an antiracist*. One World-Random House.

Kubic, C. (2021, March 3). *Can teachers be warm during a pandemic?* Edutopia. https://www.edutopia.org/article/can-teachers-be-warm-demanders-during-pandemic

Jones, W., Berg, J., & Osher, D. (2018). *Trauma and learning policy initiative (TLPI): Trauma-sensitive schools descriptive study. Final report*. American Institutes for Research.

Learning Policy Institute & Turnaround for Children. (2021). *Design principles for schools: Putting the science of learning and development into action*. https://turnaround.ams3.digitaloceanspaces.com/wp-content/uploads/2021/07/23124616/SoLD_Design_Principles_REPORT.pdf

Marzano, R. J. (2007). *The art and science of teaching*. ASCD.

Maslow, A. H. (1943). A theory of human motivation. *Psychological Review, 50*(4), 370–396. https://doi.org/10.1037/h0054346

Murray, S. (2022). *The guide to equity literacy*. www.equitymattersconsulting.org

Palardy, J. M. (1969). What teachers believe—What children achieve. *The Elementary School Journal, 69*(7), 370–374.

Rimm-Kaufman, S., & Sandilos, L. (2015, March). *Improving students' relationships with teachers to provide essential support for learning*. American Psychological Association. https://www.apa.org/education-career/k12/relationships

Ristuccia, J. (2018). The impact of trauma on learning part 3: Relationships trauma and learning policy initiative [Video]. *YouTube*. https://www.youtube.com/watch?v=to8MhwP8zZQ

Senge, P. M. (2006). *The fifth discipline: The art and practice of the learning organization*. Crown Business.

Singleton, G. E., & Linton, C. (2006). *Courageous conversations about race. A field guide for achieving equity in schools*. Corwin.

Staats, C. (2015–2016). Understanding implicit bias-what educators should know. *American Educator*. Winter 2015–2016. https://www.aft.org/sites/default/files/ae_winter2015staats.pdf

Thomsen, B., & Ackermann, E. (2015, April 13). Whole child development is undervalued. *Edutopia*. https://www.edutopia.org/blog/changemakers-whole-child-development-undervalued-bo-stjerne-thomsen-edith-ackermann

Wright, A. (1995). *The beginner's guide to colour psychology*. Kyle Cathie Limited.

Wright, A. (1998). *The beginner's guide to colour psychology*. Colour Affects Limited.

Chapter 3

Alozie, N., Haugabook Pennock, P., Madden, K., Zaidi, S., Harris, C. J., & Krajcik, J. S. (2018, March). *Designing and developing NGSS-aligned formative assessment tasks to promote equity*. Paper presented at the annual conference of National Association for Research in Science Teaching, Atlanta, GA.

Alozie, N., Lundh, H., Yang, H., & Parker, C. E. (2021). *Designing for diversity part 2. The equity and inclusion framework for curriculum design*. National Comprehensive Center.

ANET. (2021, November 29). The impact of investing an entire school community in the teaching and learning cycle. *Teaching & Learning Cycle graphic*, 2. https://www.achievementnetwork.org/anetblog/2021/12/1/teaching-learning-cycle

Assessment Network. (n.d.). *Returning to school, assessment briefs, infographics*. https://www.assessmentnetwork.net/blog/epic-demic-assessment-after-the-interlude/toolbox/assessment-briefs-and-infographics/

Bishop, R. S. (1990). Mirrors, windows and sliding glass doors. *Perspectives: Choosing and Using Books for the Classroom*, *6*(3). ix–xi.

Blackburn, B. (2008). *Rigor is not a four-letter word*. Eye On Education.

Blake, B. (1967). I taught Stripe how to whistle. *Cartoon From the Tiger Series*. https://www.teachingtimes.com/do-we-really-know-when-teaching-leads-to-learning/

DuFour, R., DuFour, R., Eaker, R., & Many, T. (2010). *Learning by doing: A handbook for professional learning communities at work*. Solution Tree Press.

Elsworth, S. (2020). *The definition of curriculum alignment*. https://classroom.synonym.com/definition-curriculum-alignment-6616423.html

Feldman, J. (2019). *Grading for equity: What it is, why it matters, and how it can transform schools and classrooms*. Corwin.

Fisher, D., & Frey, N. (2020, December 14). 3 Aspects of comprehension instruction. *Corwin Connect*. https://corwin-connect.com/2020/12/3-aspects-of-comprehension-instruction/

Florida Education Foundation. (1984). *K12 Florida school standards*. https://www.floridaeducationfoundation.org/standards

Greenstein, L. (2020). *Assessment literacy*. https://www.assessmentnetwork.net

Greenstein, L. (2020). Returning to school, assessment briefs, infographics. *Assessment Network*. https://www.assessmentnetwork.net/blog/epic-demic-assessment-after-the-interlude/toolbox/assessment-briefs-and-infographics/

Greenstein, L., & Burke, M. (2020). *Student engaged assessment strategies to empower all learners*. Rowman & Littlefield.

Hanushek, E. A., & Rivkin, S. G. (2010). Generalizations about using value-added measures of teacher quality. *American Economic Review*, *100*(2), 267–271. http://hanushek.stanford.edu/sites/default/files/publications/Hanushek%2BRivkin%202010%20AER%20100(2).pdf

Hart, H. (2021, May 13). Giving feedback: 5 elements of a more inclusive approach. *Forbes*. https://www.forbes.com/sites/hannahart/2021/05/13/giving-feedback-5-elements-of-a-more-inclusive-approach/?sh=5f39423b37fa

Hartl, S., & Riley, C. (2021, March 25). High-quality curriculum as a transformation tool for equity. Taking real steps for equity. *ASCD Express*, *16*(1). www.ascd.org/ascdexpress

Hattie, J. A., & Donoghue, G. M. (2016). Learning strategies: A synthesis and conceptual model. *NPJ Science of Learning*, 1, article 16013. https://doi.org/10.1038/npjscilearn.2016.13

Hough, L. (2019, Summer). Grade expectations: Why we need to rethink grading in our schools. *Harvard Magazine*. https://issuu.com/harvardeducation/docs/summer_2019_ed._magazine

Kane, T. J., Owens, A. M., Marinell, W. H., Daniel, R. C., Thal, D. R., & Staiger, D. O. (2016). *Teaching higher: Educators' perspectives on common core implementation*. Harvard University Center for Education Policy Research. http://cepr.harvard.edu/files/cepr/files/teaching-higher-report.pdf?m=1454988762

Muir, T. (2021, October 22). How to align curriculum and still empower teachers to teach their own way. *We Are Teachers*. https://www.weareteachers.com/avoid-curricular-chaos/

Munoz, M., & Guskey, T. (2015). Standards-based grading and reporting will improve education. *Kappan*, *96*(7), 64–68.

Murray, S., & Turner, G. (2021). *A five-course framework for accelerated learning*. www.equitymattersconsulting.org

Organization for Economic Co-Operation and Development (OECD). (2021, May 11). *Adapting curriculum to bridge equity gaps: Towards an inclusive curriculum*. OECD Publishing. https://doi.org/10.1787/6b49e118-e

Rogan, P. (2017, June 5). *Curriculum alignment: What to look for when evaluating educational resources*. Edmentum. https://blog.edmentum.com/curriculum-alignment-what-look-when-evaluating-educational-resources

Samuel, A. (2019, September 19). Why an equitable curriculum matters. *NWEA*. https://www.nwea.org/blog/2019/why-an-equitable-curriculum-matters/

Schmidt, W., Burroughs, N., Zoido, P., & Houang, R. (2015). The role of schooling in perpetuating educational inequality: An international perspective. *Educational Researcher*, *44*(7), 371–386.

Squires, D. (2012). Curriculum alignment research suggests that alignment can improve student achievement. *The Clearing House: A Journal of Educational Strategies, Issues, and Ideas*, *85*(4), 129–135.

Suskie, L. (2000, Spring) Fair assessment practices. *American Association for Higher Education (AAHE) Bulletin*, 14. https://citeseerx.ist.psu.edu/viewdoc/download?doi=10.1.1.540.9919&rep=rep1&type=pdf

The Education Hub. (2020, March 10). *Principles of assessment*. https://theeducationhub.org.nz/principles-of-assessment/

The Education Trust. (2015). *Checking in: Do classroom assignments reflect today's higher standards*. http://edtrust.org/wp-content/uploads/2014/09/CheckingIn_TheEducationTrust_Sept20152.pdf

VanTassel-Baska, J. (2017). *Introduction to the integrated curriculum model*. In J. VanTassel-Baska & C. A. Little (Eds.), *Content-based curriculum for high-Ability learners* (3rd ed.). Routledge. https://doi.org/10.4324/9781003233824

Wiggins, G. (2013). Seven keys to effective feedback. *Educational Leadership*, *70*(1), 10–16. https://pdo.ascd.org/lmscourses/PD13OC005/media/FormativeAssessmentandCCSwithELALiteracyMod_3-Reading2.pdf

Chapter 4

Bland, D. (2011). Marginalized students and insider knowledge. In G. Czerniawski & W. Kidd (Eds.), *The student voice handbook: Bridging the academic/practitioner divide* (pp. 389–397). Emerald Group.

Bland, K. D. (2012). Relationship of collaborative school culture and school achievement. *Electronic Theses and Dissertations, 785.* https://digitalcommons.georgiasouthern.edu/etd/785

Boykin, A., & Bailey, C. (2000). *The role of cultural factors in school relevant cognitive functioning: Description of home environmental factors, cultural orientations, and learning preferences. Report No. 43.* https://eric.ed.gov/?id=ED441880

Caruthers, L. E., & Friend, J. I. (2016). *Great expectations: What kids want from our urban public schools.* Information Age.

Delpit, L. (1988). The silenced dialogue: Power and pedagogy in educating other people's children. *Harvard Educational Review. 58*(3), 280–299.

Demetriou, H. A. (2019). More reasons to listen: Learning lessons from pupil voice for psychology and education. *International Journal of Student Voice, 5*(3). https://ijsv.psu.edu/article/more-reasons-to-listen-learning-lessons-from-pupil-voice-for-psychology-and-education/

Fletcher, A. (2015, February 2). *Ladder of student involvement.* SoundOut. https://soundout.org/ladder-of-student-involvement/

Gillett-Swan, J., & Sargeant, J. (2018). Assuring children's human right to freedom of opinion and expression in education. *International Journal of Speech-Language Pathology, 20*(1), 120–127. https://doi.org/10.1080/17549507.2018.1385852

Hajdukova, E. B., Hornby, G., & Cushman, P. (2016). Bullying experiences of students with social, emotional and behavioral difficulties (SEBD). *Educational Review, 68*(2), 207–221. https://doi.org/10.1080/00131911.2015.1067880

Lundy, L. (2007). Voice is not enough: Conceptualizing article 12 of the United Nations convention on the rights of the child. *British Educational Research Journal, 33*(6), 927–942. https://doi.org/10.1080/01411920701657033

Mitra, D. L. (2009). Student voice and student roles in education policy and policy reform. In G. Skyes, B. Schneider, & D. N. Plank (Eds.), *Handbook of education policy research* (pp. 819–830). Taylor & Francis.

Murray, S., & Turner, G. (2021). *A five-course framework for accelerated learning.* www.equitymattersconsulting.org

Pazey, B. (2021). Incorporating the voices and insights of students with disabilities: Let's consider our approach. *International Journal of Student Voice,* 8. https://ijsv.psu.edu/article/incorporating-the-voices-and-insights-of-students-with-disabilities-lets-consider-our-approach/

St. John, K., & Briel, L. (2017, April). *Student voice: A growing movement within education that benefits students and teachers.* Center on Transition Innovations. https://centerontransition.org/publications/download.cfm?id=61

Vander Ark, T. (2015, December 22). 10 tips for developing student agency. *Smart Agency.* https://www.gettingsmart.com/2015/12/22/201512tips-for-developing-student-agency/

Chapter 5

Albertus Magnus College. (n.d.). *Educational equity.* Center for Teaching and Learning Excellence. https://www.albertus.edu/academicservices/ctle/educational-equity/

Alsalhi, N. (2020). The effects of the use of the know-want-learn strategy on fourth-grade students' achievement in science at primary stage and their attitudes towards it. *EURASIA Journal of Mathematics, Science, and Technology Education*, *16*(4). https://doi.org/10.29333/ejmste/115165

Askell-Williams, H., Lawson, M., & Skrzypiec, G. (2012). Scaffolding cognitive and metacognitive strategy instruction in regular lessons. *Instructional Science*, *40*, 413–443. https://doi.org/10.1007/s11251-011-9182-5

Barnes, M. A. (2007). Where there's a will there's a way to close achievement gaps for children with special education needs. *Research paper published in proceedings of the 2nd research symposium Ontario ministry of education* (p. 3). www.edu.gov.on.ca/eng/research/barnes.pdf

Barrett, L. (2018, October 2). 20 ways to bring more equity to your literacy instruction. *We Are Teachers*. https://www.weareteachers.com/equity-literacy/

Belafi, C., Hwa, Y., & Kaffenberger, M. (2020). Building on solid foundations: Prioritizing universal, early, conceptual and procedural mastery of foundational skills. *RISE Insight Series*. https://doi.org/10.35489/BSG-RISE-RI_2020/021

Blackburn, B. (2017, March 29). *Special needs students: Maintain rigor! edCircuit*. https://edcircuit.com/special-needs-students-maintain-rigor/?utm_campaign=coschedule&utm_source=twitter&utm_medium=MindRocketMedia&utm_content=Special%20Needs%20Students:%20Maintain%20Rigor%20In%20Instruction!%20%7C%20edCircuit

Bostic, Q. (2021). *Text analysis toolkit*. https://achievethecore.org/page/3369/text-analysis-toolkit

Branstetter, R. (2020, October 19). *How teachers can help students with special needs navigate distance learning*. https://greatergood.berkeley.edu/article/item/how_teachers_can_help_students_with_special_needs_navigate_distance_learning

Brown, R. (2016, November 3). Tiers 2 and 3: What is the difference? *Illuminate Education*. https://www.illuminateed.com/blog/2016/11/tiers-2-and-3-what-is-the-difference/

Bullmaster-Day, M. (2021, October 1). *What is productive struggle in the classroom?* Houghton Mifflin Harcourt. https://www.hmhco.com/blog/what-is-productive-struggle

Clark, S. (2022, March 1). *Prioritizing educational equity for students with disabilities*. https://www.bestcolleges.com/blog/ways-to-prioritize-educational-equity/

Cook, S., & Rao, K. (2018). Systematically applying UDL to effective practices for students with learning disabilities. *Learning Disability Quarterly*, *41*(3), 179–191.

Davis, L. (2018). *Effective communication*. http://www.kellybear.com/TeacherArticles/TeacherTip15.html

Edmonds, R. (1982, February 25). *Programs for school improvement: An overview*. Paper presented at the National invitational conference, "Research on Teaching: Implications for practice" (Warrenton, VA, February 25–27, 1982). For related documents, see SP 021 097-107 and ED 218 257.

Foorman, B., Beyler, N., Borradaile, K., Coyne, M., Denton, C. A., Dimino, J., Furgeson, J., Hayes, L., Henke, J., Justice, L., Keating, B., Lewis, W., Sattar, S., Streke, A., Wagner, R., & Wissel, S. (2016). *Foundational skills to support reading for understanding in kindergarten through 3rd grade* (NCEE 2016-4008). National Center for Education Evaluation and Regional Assistance (NCEE), Institute of Education Sciences, U.S. Department of Education. http://whatworks.ed.gov

Franks, L. E. (2020, November 1). *Equity in literacy instruction*. National Association of Elementary School Principals (NAESP) Resources. https://www.naesp.org/resource/equity-in-literacy-instruction/

Fuchs, L., Gilbert, J., Powell, S., Cirino, P., Fuchs, D., Hamlett, C., Seethaler, P., & Tolar, T. (2016). The role of cognitive processes, foundational math skill, and calculation accuracy and fluency in word-problem solving versus pre-algebraic knowledge. *Developmental Psychology*, *52*(12), 2085–2089. https://doi.org/10.1037/dev0000227

Gellert, J. (2020). *Beware the quick fix in schools*. Center for Integrated Training & Education. https://www.citeonline.com/beware-quick-fix-schools/

Gentilucci, J. (2004). Improving school learning: The student perspective. *The Educational Forum*, *68*, 133–143.

Hammersley, M., & Woods, P. (Eds.). (1984). *Life in school: The sociology of pupil culture*. Open University Press.

Hammond, Z. (2013). *The ready for rigor framework*. https://crtandthebrain.com/wp-content/uploads/READY-FOR-RIGOR_Final.pdf

Hanen Centre. (2016). *Critical thinking: The key foundation for language and literacy success*. http://www.hanen.org/Helpful-Info/Early-Literacy-Corner/Critical-Thinking.aspx

Hotez, E. (2021, August 30). *One of us: Combating stigma against people with intellectual and developmental disabilities*. https://www.psychologicalscience.org/observer/one-of-us

Lemov, D. (2021). *Teach like a champion 3.0: 63 techniques that put on the path to college*. Jossey-Bass.

Meyer, A., Rose, D. H., & Gordon, D. (2014). *Universal design for learning: Theory and practice*. CAST.

Murray, S. (2022). Serving equitable instruction. *Where to Begin?* www.equitymattersconsulting.org

Murray, S., & Turner, G. (2021). *A five-course framework for accelerated learning*. www.equitymattersconsulting.org

Myers, K. (2016). Universal instructional design checklist: Does your curriculum provide an inclusive environment? Is it Universal instruction design (UDI) friendly? *St. Louis University MCATE conference*. https://www.mnsu.edu/globalassets/accessibility-resources/universal-instructional-design-curriculum-checklist1.pdf

Illuminate Education. (2021). *MTSS essentials: Data-informed decisions to support each student*. e-book. https://www.illuminateed.com/download/mtss-essentials-data-informed-decisions-to-support-each-student/?utm_source=Website%3A+MTSS+Solution+Page&utm_medium=Website&utm_content=Resources+-+DL+MTSS+eBook&utm_campaign=2020+Website+Updates

Jiban, C. (2020, June 25). *Let' talk equity: Reading levels, scaffolds, and grade-level text*. Northwest Evaluation Association (NWEA). https://www.nwea.org/blog/2020/equity-in-reading-levels-scaffolds-and-grade-level-text/

Joseph, M. (2020, January 3). *Supporting student productive struggle*. https://www.teachbetter.com/blog/supporting-student-productive-struggle/

Kennedy, J. (2019, July 23). *Intellectual preparation: What we've learned*. Charter School Growth Fund. https://stories.chartergrowthfund.org/intellectual-prep-what-weve-learned-5ce0506e03f9

Lapointe, S., & Klausen, C. (2021). *Foundational skills needed and what social sciences and humanities need to know. Impact research*. The/La Collaborative. McMaster University. https://macsphere.mcmaster.ca/handle/11375/26187

Lismayanti, D., & Riswanto, R. (2014). The effect of using the KWL (Know, Want, Learned) strategy on EFL students' reading comprehension achievement. *International Journal of Humanities and Social Science, 4*(7), 225–233.

Marco Learning. (2018, August 27). *Teacher bias: The elephant in the classroom*. https://marcolearning.com/teacher-bias-the-elephant-in-the-classroom/

McElhone, D. (2014). *Text talk: Engaging readers in purposeful discussion*. International Reading Association. https://www.literacyworldwide.org/docs/default-source/member-benefits/e-ssentials/ila-e-ssentials-8045.pdf

Montgomery County Public Schools (MCPS). (2010). *Equitable classroom practices: A resource for equitable classroom practices*. Montgomery County Public Schools. https://www.montgomeryschoolsmd.org/departments/development/resources/ecp/

Muhammad, G. (2020). *Cultivating genius: An equity framework for cultivating and historically responsive literacy*. Scholastic.

National Council of Teachers of Mathematics. (2014). *Principles to action: Executive summary*. NCTM. https://www.nctm.org/uploadedFiles/Standards_and_Positions/PtAExecutiveSummary.pdf

National Council of Teachers of Mathematics. (2018b). *Catalyzing change in high school mathematics: Initiating critical conversations*. NCTM.

Nichols, M. (2008). *Talking about text: Guiding students to increase comprehension through purposeful talk*. Shell Education.

Nicol, J. (2017, December 8). *Removing systemic barriers in education*. The Universal Design for Learning (UDL) Project. https://www.theudlproject.com/blog/removing-systemic-barriers-in-education

Ogle, D. M. (1986). KWL: A teaching model that develops active reading of the expository text. *The Reading Teacher, 39*, 564–570.

Open University. (2008). *Thinking critically*. The Open University.

Palinscar, A. (1986). The role of dialogue in providing scaffolding instruction. *Educational Psychologist, 21*(1&2), 73–98.

Picard, D. (2022). *Teaching students with disabilities*. Vanderbilt University. https://cft.vanderbilt.edu/guides-sub-pages/disabilities/

Ralabate, P. K. (2011, August 30). Universal design for learning: Meeting the needs of all students. *The ASHA Leader*. https://www.readingrockets.org/article/universal-design-learning-meeting-needs-all-students

Reutzel, R. (2020, June 11). *What is close reading and how can you effectively teach it*. Curriculum Associates. https://www.curriculumassociates.com/blog/how-to-teach-close-reading.

Research on Improving Systems of Education (RISE). (2020, August 6). *Building on solid foundations: Prioritizing universal, early, conceptual, and procedural mastery of foundational skills.* https://riseprogramme.org/publications/building-solid-foundations-prioritising-universal-early-conceptual-and-procedural

Schalock, H. D., Schalock, M. D., Cowart, B., & Myton, D. (1993). Extending teacher assessment beyond knowledge and skills: An emerging focus on teacher accomplishments. *Journal of Personnel Evaluation in Education, 7*, 105–133.

Schoenfeld, A. (2016). *The teaching for robust understanding project: The teaching for robust understanding (TRU) observation guide for mathematics: A tool for teachers, coaches, administrators, and professional learning communities.* Graduate School of Education, University of California. http://TRUframework.org

Schoenfeld, A. (2020, March 10). *How can teachers help students who lack foundational math skills but have been passed into advanced math classes? Brief 006.* The Answer Lab at the University of Southern California. https://theanswerlab.rossier.usc.edu/wp-content/uploads/2020/03/AnswerLab_Issue6_main-031020-FINAL.pdf

Smith, M., & Stein, M. (2018). *5 Practices for orchestrating productive mathematics discussions* (2nd ed.). National Council of Teachers of Mathematics, Corwin.

Spencer, S. (2011). Universal design in learning: Assistance for teachers in today's inclusive classrooms. *Interdisciplinary Journal of Teaching and Learning, 1*(1), 10–22.

Spooner, F., Baker, J., Harris, A., Ahlgrim-Delzell, L., & Browder, D. (2007). Effects of training in universal design for learning on lesson plan development. *Remedial and Special Education, 28*(2), 105–116.

Tanner, K. D. (2012). Promoting student metacognition. *CBE-life Sciences Education, 11*, 113–120. https://www.improvewithmetacognition.com/promoting-student-metacognition/

Toth, M. (2021, April 1). *Instructional equity and access in a pandemic.* National School Boards Association (NSBA). https://nsba.org/ASBJ/2021/April/instructional-equity-access-pandemic#:~:text=Instructional%20equity%20means%20that%20every,student%20is%20learning%20the%20lesson

Tracey, K. (2013, October 21). Writing to read: Evidence for how writing can improve reading. *Literacy Now.* International Literacy Association. https://www.literacyworldwide.org/blog/literacy-now/2013/10/21/writing-to-read-evidence-for-how-writing-can-improve-reading

Tucker, C., Wycoff, J., & Green, J. (2017). *Blended learning in action: A practical guide to sustainable change.* Corwin.

University of Waterloo Centre for Teaching Excellence. (n.d.). *Teaching problem-solving skills.* https://uwaterloo.ca/centre-for-teaching-excellence/teaching-resources/teaching-tips/developing-assignments/cross-discipline-skills/teaching-problem-solving-skills

Wabisabi Learning. (n.d.). *The critical thinking skills cheat sheet.* https://wabisabilearning.com/blogs/critical-thinking/critical-thinking-skills-cheatsheet-infographic.

Wilburne, J., & Peterson, W. (2007). Using a before-during-after (BDA) model to plan effective secondary mathematics lessons. *Mathematics Teacher: Learning and Teaching PK–12, 101*, 209–213.

Chapter 6

Anderson-Butcher, D., Amorose, A., Lachini, A., & Ball, A. (2013). *Community and youth collaborative institute school experience family of surveys: Elementary School Student Survey.* College of Social Work, the Ohio State University.

Ashwin, P., & McVitty, D. (2015). The meanings of student engagement: Implications for policies and practices. In A. Curaj, L. Matei, R. Pricopie, J. Salmi, & P. Scott (Eds.), *The European higher education area.* Springer. https://doi.org/10.1007/978-3-319-20877-0_23. https://www.viewsonic.com/library/education/what-is-student-engagement

Bates, A. W. (2015). *Chapter 8: Choosing and using media in education: The SECTIONS model. From teaching in a digital age. A creative commons attribution-non commercial 4.0 international license.* http://opentextbc.ca/teachinginadigitalage/

Blackburn, B. (n.d.). *How technology can increase Rigor in the classroom.* Teach Thought. https://www.teachthought.com/pedagogy/rigor-in-the-classroom/TeachThought

Bolden, F. (2019, August 16). How technology can increase student engagement. *Teach Hub.* https://www.teachhub.com/technology-in-the-classroom/2019/08/how-technology-can-increase-student-engagement/#:~:text=Teachers%20can%20use%20technology%20to,bold%20text%20of%20difficult%20words

Bond, M., & Bedenlier, S. (2019). Facilitating student engagement through educational technology: Towards a conceptual framework. *Journal of Interactive Media in Education, 2019*(1), 11.

CAYCI. (2015). *Community and youth collaborative institute school experience survey for elementary students.* https://www.cayci.osu.edu/wp-content/uploads/2015/01/2015-CAYCI_Elementary_Survey_FINAL.pdf

Dahl, R. (1964). *Charlie and the chocolate factory.* Penguin, Random House.

Dale, E. (1969). *Audio-visual methods in teaching* (3rd ed., p. 108). Holt, Rinehart & Winston.

Davis, B. G. (1993). *Tools for teaching.* Jossey-Bass Publishers.

EdWeek Research Center. (2021, January 6). *Data Snapshot: What teacher and student morale looks like right now.* https://www.edweek.org/leadership/data-snapshot-what-teacher-and-student-morale-looks-like-right-now/2021/01

Fredricks, J. A., Blumenfeld, P. C., & Paris, A. H. (2004). School engagement: Potential of the concept, state of the evidence. *Review of Educational Research, 74*(1), 59–109. https://doi.org/10.3102/00346543074001059

Gallup Inc. (2019). *Education technology use in schools.* https://www.newschools.org/wp-content/uploads/2020/03/Gallup-Ed-Tech-Use-in-Schools-2.pdf

Gregory, A., & Skiba, R. J. (2019). Reducing suspension and increasing equity through supportive and engaging schools. In J. A. Fredricks, A. L. Reschly, & S. L. Christenson (Eds.), *Handbook of student engagement interventions: Working with disengaged students* (pp. 121–134). Elsevier Academic Press. https://doi.org/10.1016/B978-0-12-813413-9.00009-7

Hanover Research. (2020). *Virtual engagement toolkit.* https://insights.hanoverresearch.com/hubfs/Virtual-Student-Engagement-Toolkit.pdf?utm_campaign=Confirmation%20Emails&utm_medium=email&_hsmi=60616640&_hsenc=p2ANqtz-9RXIAsbhgqwAEcYzZd15C5OPaAcWRTd3cFs-

qZOJgVojiBlgCNM2D2ciNec8j625JI_gJtza1bLMMJ5wU7iWFKZzukorpB5epjskdgxx1yCJCE8kU
&utm_content=60616640&utm_source=hs_automation

Kieschnick, W. (2022, May 10). *Connections: The educator's atlas–Why engagement matters.* https://www.connectedd.org/blog/connections-the-educators-atlas-why-engagement-matters

McKenna, M., & Kear, D. (1990). Measuring attitudes towards reading: A new tool for teachers. *The Reading Teacher, 43*(8), 626–639.

Murray, S., & Turner, G. (2021). *A five-course framework for accelerated learning.* www.equitymattersconsulting.org

Noguera, P. (2015, September 15). Pedro Noguera examines how student engagement impacts student achievement. *Edthena.* (PowerPoint). https://www.youtube.com/watch?v=Sz0o6lI7dnE

Noguera, P. (2020). *Student engagement is the pathway to achievement.* https://pltogether.org/student-engagement-is-the-pathway-to-achievement/

Puentedura, R. (2006). *Transformation, technology, and education.* http://hippasus.com/resources/tte/

Puentedura, R. (2014). *SAMR and TPCK: A hands-on approach to classroom practice.* Hipassus. En ligne. http://www.-hippasus.com/rrpweblog/archives/2012/09/03/BuildingUponSA-M-R.pdf

Punya, M., & Koehler, M. (2006). Technological pedagogical content knowledge: A framework for teacher knowledge. *Teachers College Record, 108*(6), 1017–1054.

Recht, D. R., & Leslie, L. (1988). Effect of prior knowledge on good and poor readers' memory of text. *Journal of Educational Psychology, 80*(1), 16–20. https://doi.org/10.1037/0022-0663.80.1.16

Reckmeyer, M. (2019, October 30). *Focus on student engagement for better achievement.* Gallup. https://www.gallup.com/education/267521/focus-student-engagement-better-academic-outcomes.aspx

Ristuccia, J. (2018). The impact of trauma on learning part 3: Relationships trauma and learning policy initiative [Video]. YouTube. https://www.youtube.com/watch?v=to8MhwP8zZQ

Seif, E. (2018, November 16). *Dimensions of deep learning: Levels of engagement and learning.* https://www.ascd.org/blogs/dimensions-of-deep-learning-levels-of-engagement-and-learning

Teach and Kids Learn. (2017, November 16). *Increasing deep student engagement and motivation.* https://www.teachnkidslearn.com/increasing-deep-student-engagement/

Theobald, M. A. (2006). *Increasing student motivation: Strategies for middle and high school teachers.* Corwin.

Toth, M. (2021, March 17). Why student engagement is important in a post-COVID world –and 5 strategies to improve it. *Learning Sciences International.* https://www.learningsciences.com/blog/why-is-student-engagement-important/

Wilcox, L. (2018, June 4). *NBPTS top 5 strategies for motivating students.* National Board for Professional Teaching Standards (NBPTS). https://www.nbpts.org/blog/top-5-strategies-for-motivating-students

INDEX

A SAGE Publishing Company

Helping educators make the greatest impact

CORWIN HAS ONE MISSION: to enhance education through intentional professional learning.

We build long-term relationships with our authors, educators, clients, and associations who partner with us to develop and continuously improve the best evidence-based practices that establish and support lifelong learning.